Janet Malcolm's previous books include *In the Freud Archives, Psychoanalysis: The Impossible Profession* (both published by Granta Books) and *The Silent Woman: Sylvia Plath and Ted Hughes.* Her most recent book is the highly acclaimed *Reading Chekhov: A Critical Journey* (Granta Books). Born in Prague, she grew up in New York, where she lives with her husband, Gardner Botsford.

Ian Jack is the editor of *Granta* magazine. Previously he was the editor of the *Independent on Sunday.* He has been a journalist since 1965, when he began his career as a reporter on a small weekly newspaper in Scotland.

Also by Janet Malcolm

THE JOURNALIST AND THE MURDERER

Janet Malcolm

Introduction by Ian Jack

Granta Books

London

Granta Publications, 2/3 Hanover Yard, London N1 8BE

This edition published in Great Britain by Granta Books 2004
First published in the US by Alfred A. Knopf, Inc., 1990

A CIP catalogue record for this book is available from the British Library.

3 5 7 9 10 8 6 4 2

Printed and bound in Great Britain by Mackays of Chatham plc

To Andulka

So a novelist is the same as a journalist, then. Is that what you're saying?

Introduction

Given its title and given its splendidly provocative first sentence, this book could easily be mistaken for a treatise on modern journalism. In fact, while the practice of journalism lies at its narrative heart – in its different way it ranks with Evelyn Waugh's novel, *Scoop*, as one of the wisest descriptions of the subject, sometimes even rivalling Waugh in its comedy – *The Journalist and the Murderer* illuminates many other human concerns, chief among them the frequent impossibility of ever knowing the truth about other people, or ourselves. The practice of the law, the practice of psychology, the practice of interviewing, researching and writing, the practice of friendship, the practice of art – all these things are profoundly questioned by Janet Malcolm in the course of her story and her scrutiny of what, altogether, might be described as the practice of the personality: how we express and deploy it for our own ends, deliberately or unknowingly. In a book of around only one hundred and sixty pages, Malcolm's is a remarkable achievement. Her insights are both original and disquieting, and (or so it seems to me, as a journalist) usually hit the nails of our imperfect, sometimes rotten, behaviour bang on the head.

I write 'usually' above because the one sentence in this book that I would quarrel with – and many others, particularly journalists, have objected to – is the first and most famous: 'Every journalist who is not too stupid or too full of himself to notice what is going on knows that what he does is morally indefensible.' This sentence is followed by: 'He is a kind of confidence man, preying on people's vanity, ignorance, or loneliness.' Can that really be? Every journalist, all kinds of journalism? The foreign correspondent at the scene of the flood, the court-reporter, the fashion writer, the stock analyst? Their work may be flawed and inadequate. It may even, in the case of the share-tipper, be corrupt. But it is hard to see what they do, always and universally, as 'morally indefensible'. Malcolm wrote (and still writes) for the *New Yorker*, where the pieces that became this book were first published. Perhaps she was tired of the *New Yorker*'s tradition of information-laden first paragraphs, neutral in tone, which 'set the scene'. Perhaps there was an Austenite inside her struggling to get out; 'It is a truth universally acknowledged … ' and so on (in which case it would be absurd to quibble with it – '*Universally*,' Miss Austen, 'even among pederasts with good fortunes, or among the heathen races?')

Is it no more than that? A bold writerly stroke, rhetoric to wake up the reader, not to be examined too carefully for its word-by-word sense? An import from another literary form such as fiction? I don't think so for a moment. Malcolm is a writer of great precision – luminous in her description of the divide between fiction and non-fiction and their different contracts with the reader. But here a kind of anger seems to be at work which has led her to over-generalize from her own experience. The anger in the sentence comes, I think, from self-reproach as well as the reproach of others. What Malcolm means – though what a dull opening sentence it might make if more carefully expressed – is that a particular form of journalism (or book writing, or television documentary) relies on the 'journalist-subject' relationship, which Malcolm later describes as 'the canker that lies at the heart of the rose of journalism'. Every reporter who talks to human beings for his information has such relationships, of course, but they are often brief and impersonal: questions put, answers offered (or not), the telephone put back in its cradle. A 'canker' may exist even here. Over the course of a five-minute conversation the journalist may pretend that he is on his subject's 'side' (when he isn't), or he may distort or exaggerate what his subject has said so that it better fits his narrative, or makes a more lively or alarming story. (As I write this, in September 2003, the latter possibility is one of the main questions facing the public inquiry into the death of David Kelly, the British government scientist and expert on Iraqi weapons who was the source of a BBC report which claimed that political associates of the Prime Minister had 'sexed-up' the intelligence dossier that made the case for war against Iraq.) For the canker to do its worst work, however, it needs a different, more artful, and altogether more ambitious form of writing in which to flourish.

The form can go under several names: literary reportage, extended reporting, the long profile, or simply the 'big piece'. In some ways 'journalism' – implying something written quickly for a short public life in newsprint – is a misleading overall description of the form. It exists in books ('the non-fiction novel') and on film as well as in magazines, and it can take months, even years, to produce. Often what it tries to do is to reveal the 'truth' of a complicated situation or human predicament by going beyond the quick superficialities of most other reporting, digging deeper into other lives. Because the reporter needs to know his subjects, he will need to befriend them or at least not turn them into close-mouthed, unapproachable enemies. He will want them to trust him, which means he may need them to think that in the end his words will serve their characters, behaviour and views sympathetically, or with what they imagine to be justice. And in this he – or she – will often disappoint them.

When she came to write this story, Janet Malcolm was already one of the world's finest practitioners of this kind of research and writing, and had come to understand its imperatives and moral dangers: the need to make a story that satisfies its author and his or her idea of the truth rather than that of the story's human subjects; the consequently sometimes sacrificed subject, who is impaled on the 'text's necessities'; the fool's gold of 'objectivity'. Bringing these insights to bear, Malcolm not only tells a gripping, cautionary story of personal manipulation and betrayal, she also makes us see the strings being pulled behind her telling of it. 'There but for the grace of God …' many journalists will feel, squirming at the court-room disclosures of the writer Joe McGinniss's deceit of the murderer, Jeffrey MacDonald. But they – as well as any other reader – will also feel that Malcolm has needed the grace of God herself, and perhaps that it has occasionally failed her. The temptations of the real-life story are never far away from Malcolm's alert conscience; the story down the ages, inviting both the writer and his subject towards it with its glittering baubles (money! reputation! some clear order distilled from the opaque complexity of life!).

But who is this wise person, the narrator of this story, the 'I' of this book? In the afterword, Malcolm has this to say about first-person narrators in journalism:

'This character is unlike all the journalist's other characters in that he forms the exception to the rule that nothing may be invented: the "I" character in journalism is almost pure invention. Unlike the "I" of autobiography, who is meant to be seen as a representation of the writer, the "I" of journalism is connected to the writer only in a tenuous way – the way, say, that Superman is connected to Clark Kent. The journalistic "I" is an over-reliable narrator, a functionary to whom crucial tasks of narration and argument and tone have been entrusted, an ad-hoc creation, like the chorus of Greek tragedy. He is an emblematic figure, an embodiment of the idea of the dispassionate observer of life. Nevertheless ... among journalists, there are those who have trouble sorting themselves out from the Supermen of their texts.'

A brilliant analysis, to be stitched in embroidery and hung in the lecture halls of writing and journalism schools, though it takes us nowhere in the case of Malcolm herself. Here, a brief outline of her Clark Kent life is called for. She was born Jana Wienovera in Prague in 1935, one of two daughters of secular Jewish parents. Her father was a psychiatrist and her mother a lawyer. The family fled to the USA shortly before the Second World War. She studied at the High School of Art and Music in Manhattan and then at the University of Michigan, where she met her first husband, Donald Malcolm, who reviewed books and wrote on the theatre for the *New Yorker*. In the 1960s, she herself began writing for that magazine on interior decoration, design, and photography. She separated from her first husband (who died in 1975), and later married her editor at the *New Yorker*, Gardner Botsford. They have an apartment in Manhattan and a summer home in New England. She has a daughter and a granddaughter. She makes and exhibits collages. To encounter her is to meet – and here I hope I am not, in her words, 'committing the journalistic solecism of putting a person's feelings above a text's necessities' – the opposite of a bore or the kind of initially attractive person who eventually becomes a bore through constant self-advertisement or self-certainty. She is gentle, curious about the people she finds herself among, shrewd but not unkind, amusing. A common complaint among journalists who have interviewed her is that she is annoyingly and deliberately reticent about herself. She may be; she values privacy. But it is also possible that she distrusts simplifications of herself – even or especially those from her own lips – a distrust which makes her exceptional in an age when people so readily deliver, in her phrase, 'auto-novelised' versions of themselves for public consumption (see any chat show). She understands – too well – the twin anxieties of the interview: the interviewer's need to keep his subject talking, the interviewee's fear of being found uninteresting. As she writes in this book: '… many of the strange things that subjects say to writers – things of almost suicidal rashness – they say out of their desperate need to keep the writer's attention riveted.'

Malcolm as the 'I' on the page – or, to continue with the metaphor, as Superwoman – developed in the late 1970s after she turned away from aesthetics as a subject and the essay as a form, away from the criticism of artefacts, which can't answer back, and towards the assessment of human beings, who can. She became a reporter: she went to see people, talked to them, recorded what they said, and then skilfully composed the story which reflected the knowledge she had gained. This method lay behind her book, *Psychoanalysis: The Impossible Profession*, published in 1981, in which, over several conversations with one particular analyst, she drew out the pitfalls and difficulties of analysis as a tool of self-understanding or self-cure. She wrote not as a fierce opponent of analysis but as a sympathetic critic and knowledgeable interlocutor, and the book displayed her great gift for clarity and for subtle and ironic storytelling. Few accounts of psychoanalysis have been so directly understandable or readable without traducing the subject or hiding its complexity. In her next book, *In the Freud Archives*, published in 1984, she used her techniques to unravel a bitter quarrel that had broken out inside the profession of psychoanalysis over Sigmund Freud's intellectual legacy, and in particular how right or wrong he had been to discard his first explanation for sexual hysteria in his patients, that they had been *actually* abused as children, in favour of a second, that they had *imagined* this abuse as part of their infant sexual fantasies and Oedipal instincts. A young, flamboyant analyst, Jeffrey Masson, believed that Freud had been wrong to have revised his opinion, and in papers and interviews he attacked the orthodox Freudian beliefs of the psychoanalytic establishment. He then, unsurprisingly, lost the job he had just been given by the guardian of Freud's papers and letters in the Library of Congress and at the Freud house in London, where Freud's daughter, Anna, still lived. He sued the people who had hired him – hired him, it seemed, despite the fact that he had never kept his anti-Freudian thoughts a secret. How had such a sceptic penetrated the establishment to the extent that Freud's unpublished thoughts – unmined gold to the devout – were actually in his care? To sort all this out, Malcolm pursued the various parties involved in the quarrel, talked to them, got to know them, and then portrayed their personalities in the book, which, like most of her work, first ran as pieces in the *New Yorker*. Masson was her main character. He was outraged at her depiction, denied that he had said words that were attributed to him, and sued for libel.

The case was dismissed by a federal judge in 1987, but Masson tenaciously pursued it through courts of appeal until, in 1994, a federal jury found that Malcolm had not libelled him. Malcolm's name was cleared, but until that point the publicity surrounding the case had made her unhappy; she wondered whether in the minds of some people she would always be seen as 'a kind of fallen woman of journalism'.

When *The Journalist and the Murderer* first appeared in two *New Yorker* issues in 1989, several of Malcolm's critics put two and two together and made more than four. Malcolm, they suggested, felt guilty about Masson, and now by way of explanation or expiation she had chosen to write about a trial which laid bare the quandaries and betrayals of the journalist-subject relationship in their starkest form. At this trial, Jeffrey MacDonald, the convicted murderer of his wife and daughters, sued Joe McGinniss, who with MacDonald's active co-operation had written a book about the case, for fraud and breach of contract. MacDonald had imagined that he and McGinniss were allies and friends, and that McGinniss's book would exonerate him as an innocent and decent man. Instead, after the prolonged appearance of friendship lasting the time the writer needed MacDonald's help, McGinniss wrote about him as a murderous psychopath. Malcolm, the argument ran, was really writing about herself and Masson.

In her afterword, Malcolm dismisses this confessional, 'veiled autobiography' interpretation of this book, and it is certainly hard to believe that a writer of her intelligence and self-awareness would do anything so crude. On the other hand, it is equally hard to believe that her experience with Masson, first as a journalistic subject and then as a legal opponent, didn't inform the book in one way or another – in ways that, knowingly or unknowingly, she may not have wanted to concede.

In terms of the delights of reading her, none of this matters. Like all her work, *The Journalist and the Murderer*, is tethered pleasurably to the specific: people, times, places, letters, conversations. Rather than an over-reliable narrator, she is a thoughtful guide to human behaviour and its relationship to one of the most important aspects of modern life, the distorting mirror of the media. Her perceptions are memorably expressed. 'Something happens to people when they meet a journalist,' she writes in an early passage of this book,

> '…and what happens is exactly the opposite of what one would expect. One would think that extreme wariness and caution would be the order of the day, but in fact childish impetuosity and trust are far more common. The journalistic encounter seems to have the same regressive effect on a subject as the psychoanalytic encounter. The subject becomes a kind of child of the writer, regarding him as a permissive, all-accepting, all-forgiving mother, and expecting that the book will be written by her. Of course, the book is written by the strict, all-noticing, unforgiving father.'

Our knowledge of why we do what we do will never be complete. What Malcolm reveals to us is the glorious interestingness of the search.

Ian Jack

The Journalist
and the Murderer

EVERY journalist who is not too stupid or too full of himself to notice what is going on knows that what he does is morally indefensible. He is a kind of confidence man, preying on people's vanity, ignorance, or loneliness, gaining their trust and betraying them without remorse. Like the credulous widow who wakes up one day to find the charming young man and all her savings gone, so the consenting subject of a piece of nonfiction writing learns—when the article or book appears—*his* hard lesson. Journalists justify their treachery in various ways according to their temperaments. The more pompous talk about freedom of speech and "the public's right to know"; the least talented talk about Art; the seemliest murmur about earning a living.

The catastrophe suffered by the subject is no simple matter of an unflattering likeness or a misrepresentation of his views; what pains him, what rankles and sometimes drives him to extremes of vengefulness, is the deception that has been practiced on him. On reading the article or book in question, he has to face the fact that the journalist—who seemed so friendly and sympathetic, so keen to understand him fully, so remarkably attuned to his vision of things—never had the slightest intention of collaborating with him on his story but always intended to write a story of his own. The disparity between what seems to be the intention of an interview as it is taking place and what it actually turns out to have been in aid of always comes as a shock to the subject. His situation resembles that of the subject of Stanley Milgram's famous psychological experiment (conducted at Yale in the early sixties), who was tricked into believing that he was participating in a study of the effect of punishment on learning and memory when in fact what was being studied was his own capacity for cruelty under the pressure of authority. In an ingenious fake laboratory setup, the "naïve subject"—a volunteer who had answered an advertisement in a New Haven newspaper—was told to give an increasingly painful electric shock to a person, presumably another volunteer, in response to every wrong answer to a test question. In *Obedience to Authority*, his book about the experiment, Milgram writes of his surprise at the large number of subjects who obeyed the experimenter, and kept on pulling the lever even though the receiver of the shocks was screaming with pain—or, rather, with simulated pain, since the whole thing was rigged: the electrical apparatus to which the victim was strapped was a stage prop, and the victim himself was an actor. Milgram's idea had been to see how ordinary Americans would behave when put in a situation roughly comparable to that of the ordinary Germans who were ordered to participate actively in the destruction of the Jews of Europe. The results were not encouraging. Although a few subjects refused to go on with the experiment at the first sign of distress from the victim, most subjects docilely continued giving shock after shock. However, Milgram's chilling findings are not the point. The point lies in the *structure* of the situation: the deliberately induced delusion, followed by a moment of shattering revelation. The dizzying shift of perspective experienced by the subject of the Milgram experiment when he was "debriefed," or "dehoaxed," as Milgram calls it, is comparable to the dislocation felt by the subject of a book or article when he first reads it. The subject of the piece of writing has not suffered the tension and anxiety endured by the subject of the "Eichmann experiment" (as it has been called)—on the contrary, he has been on a sort of narcissist's holiday during the period of interviews—but when the moment of peripeteia comes, he is confronted with the same mortifying spectacle of himself flunking a test of character he did not know he was taking.

However, unlike the reader of *Obedience to Authority*, with whom Milgram shares the technical details of the deception, the reader of a work of journalism can only imagine how the writer got the subject to make such a spectacle of himself. The subject, for his part, is not likely to supply the answer. After his dehoaxing, he tends to pick himself up and walk away from the debacle, relegating his relationship with the journalist to the rubbish heap of love affairs that ended badly and are best pushed out of consciousness. Occasionally, a subject will have become so enmeshed with the journalist that he cannot let go of him, and long after the galling book has been remaindered the relationship is maintained through the interminable lawsuit that the subject launches to keep the writer bound to him. Yet even here the journalist's perfidy is not exposed, for the lawyer who takes the subject's case translates his story of seduction and betrayal into one or several of the conventional narratives of libel law, such as defamation of character or false statement of facts or reckless disregard of the truth.

IN THE summer of 1984, a lawsuit was filed by a subject against a writer in which, remarkably, the underlying narrative of betrayed love was not translated into any of those conventional narratives but, rather, was told straight—and, moreover, told so compellingly that at trial five of the six jurors were persuaded that a man who was serving three consecutive life sentences for the murder of his wife and two small children was deserving of more sympathy than the writer who had deceived him.

I learned of the case only after the trial had ended, when I received a letter, dated September 1, 1987, from a certain Daniel Kornstein. The letter—which had been sent to some thirty-odd journalists throughout the country—began:

> I am the lawyer who defended Joe McGinniss, author of *Fatal Vision*, in a six-week jury trial recently concluded in Los Angeles. As you may know, the suit was filed by convicted triple murderer Jeffrey MacDonald, the subject of McGinniss's book.
>
> The trial ended in a hung jury. Although the plaintiff recovered nothing, the possibility of a retrial means that in a very real sense the issues raised by the trial are still alive, open, and undecided. Indeed, one of the jurors—who admitted she had not read a book since high school—was reported to have said afterwards that she would have awarded "millions and millions of dollars to set an example for all authors to show they can't tell an untruth" to their subjects.

Kornstein went on to characterize the suit—which was for fraud and breach of contract—as an attempt "to set a new precedent whereby a reporter or author would be legally obligated to disclose his state of mind and attitude toward his subject during the process of writing and research," and to speak of the "grave threat to established journalistic freedoms" that such a precedent would pose:

> For the first time, a disgruntled subject has been permitted to sue a writer on grounds that render irrelevant the truth or falsity of what was published. . . . Now, for the first time, a journalist's demeanor and point of view throughout the entire creative process have become an issue to be resolved by jury trial. . . . The MacDonald claim suggests that newspaper and magazine reporters, as well as authors, can and will be sued for writing truthful but unflattering articles should they ever have acted in a fashion that indicated a sympathetic attitude toward their interview subject.

With his letter Kornstein enclosed transcripts of the testimony of William F. Buckley, Jr., and Joseph Wambaugh, who had appeared as expert witnesses for the defense, and excerpts from his own closing statement, "in which I tried to stress the gravity and scope of this new threat to freedom of expression." He concluded, "Joe McGinniss and I both feel that the danger is sufficiently clear and present as to warrant your close attention and concern."

I took Kornstein's bait—I don't know if any of the other journalists he wrote to did—and a few days later I was driving up to Williamstown, Massachusetts, to talk to Joe McGinniss at his house there. I looked forward to the interview, which would be the first of a series of tape-recorded conversations that McGinniss and I had arranged to have over the next few weeks. I had never interviewed a journalist before, and was curious about what would develop between me and a journalistically knowledgeable, rather than naïve, subject. Here, clearly, there would be none of the moral uneasiness that the naïve subject all but forces the journalist to endure as the price of his opportunity to once again point out the frailty of human nature. McGinniss and I would be less like experimenter and subject than like two experimenters strolling home from the lab together after the day's work, companionably thrashing out the problems of the profession. The tape recorder would preserve the trenchant things we would say; nobody would "do" anything to anyone. The conversation would be serious, on a high level, maybe even lively and witty.

It did not work out that way. McGinniss refused the role of co-experimenter, preferring to play the role of subject. After the first hour of the five hours we spent together, I stopped struggling to preserve my scenario of elevated talk between confrères and gave in to McGinniss's imperative that we play the old game of Confession, by which journalists earn their bread and subjects indulge their masochism. For, of course, at bottom, no subject is naïve. Every hoodwinked widow, every deceived lover, every betrayed friend, every subject of writing knows on some level what is in store for him, and remains in the relationship anyway, impelled by something stronger than his reason. That McGinniss, who had interviewed hundreds of people and knew the game backward and forward, should nevertheless exhibit himself to me as a defensive, self-righteous, scared man only demonstrates the strength of this force. Near the end of the day, he told me of a dream he had had the night before: "I was back in the courthouse in L.A. There was a second trial. I said, 'No, this can't be happening. I'm not ready for this yet,

it's too soon, I haven't recovered from the first trial yet.'
When I woke up this morning, my amateur analysis of the
dream was that it was about my talking to you today. This
would be the new trial. It didn't seem very subtle. The
message was right on the surface." At six o'clock, the tape
recorder clicked, and though McGinniss sat waiting for
me to put in a new tape, I decided to bring the interview
to an end. When, two days later, he called to cancel our
future interviews and to say "I want to put all this behind
me," I was not surprised, and rather relieved: I had begun
to sense that McGinniss's confession to me was not a new
one. Someone had been there before me, and something
was being repeated with me. A few weeks later, upon
reading the transcript of the MacDonald-McGinniss trial,
I knew who and what it was. What McGinniss had not
yet recovered from—what he had no doubt been helplessly reliving in his imagination during his meeting with
me—was a four-and-a-half-day interrogation by Gary
Bostwick, the plaintiff's lawyer. Bostwick had mauled
McGinniss until there was little left of him. What McGinniss had gone through at the trial was what one goes
through in those nightmares of being found out, from
which one awakens with tears of gratitude that it is just a
dream. Only the most hardhearted person could read the
transcript of Bostwick's examination without feeling pity
for McGinniss. But even the staunchest defender of a
journalist's right to do his work in whatever unpleasant
way he chooses cannot but wonder how McGinniss
could have been so imprudent as to leave behind—in the
form of some forty letters to MacDonald—a written
record of his bad faith.

McGINNISS is forty-eight years old and has published six books, the most recent being *Blind Faith*, of 1989. The first, *The Selling of the President, 1968*, written when he was twenty-six, brought him immediate fame and acclaim. In the 1968 Nixon-Humphrey campaign, he had penetrated the inner councils of the advertising agency hired by Nixon, and in his book he revealed the techniques by which Nixon had been made to appear less awful on television. This was in the early days of television's use in politics, and McGinniss's revelations (today very tame) seemed startling and ominous. The defeated Humphrey was quoted on the book jacket as having said, "The biggest mistake in my political life was not to learn how to use television," and "I'm fighting packaged politics. It's an abomination for a man to place himself completely in the hands of the technicians, the ghost writers, the experts, the pollsters and come out only as an attractive package."

During our talk, McGinniss spoke of how he had come to write *The Selling of the President*, and surprised me when he said that he had first taken his idea of reporting a Presidential-advertising campaign to the Humphrey camp. "Humphrey's people said, 'Are you crazy? This is all secret. The public shouldn't know about this. No way.' Humphrey's advertising agency was Doyle Dane Bernbach, a very sophisticated group who recognized right up front that a book calling attention to the process would not be in their best interest, so they wouldn't give me any access at all. Nixon's people were almost touchingly naïve. They said, 'Oh, gosh, really—a book? Yeah, sure.' These were people who had had very little experience of being written about." Then, as if the ghost of Bostwick had just appeared at his side, McGinniss added, "But I hardly felt the obligation to say when I arrived at their offices every morning, 'Gentlemen, I must again remind you that I'm a registered Democrat who plans to vote against Mr. Nixon, and that I think what you're doing—which is trying to fool the American people—is sinister and malevolent, and that I intend to portray you in terms that you are not going to find flattering.' I felt no obligation to make that statement. And when they were talking about what they were doing and turned to me and said 'What do you think of that?' I'd say 'Yeah, that looks good' if I thought it was done effectively. I was trying to make myself as unobtrusive a presence as possible. And when the book was published, they reacted with outrage or wry amusement, depending on their sense of humor or their degree of passion as Nixonians. But in no case did anyone think he could sue because he had been defrauded into believing I was going to do something other than what I did."

McGinniss's next book was a novel, *The Dream Team*, which was a critical and commercial failure. Then, in 1976, he published a curious book called *Heroes*. It is a confessional work that—like many such exercises—confesses something different from what the confessor thinks he is confessing; by making himself into a subject, the autobiographer sets himself up for a betrayal no less profound than that invited by the subject of someone else's writing. *Heroes* juxtaposes chapters about (among other personal matters) McGinniss's inability to be nice to his girlfriend, Nancy Doherty (now his second wife), because of the guilt he feels over leaving his wife and three children, with chapters about meetings with public figures such as Eugene McCarthy, Ted Kennedy, Daniel Berrigan, George McGovern, William Westmoreland, and William Styron, who disappoint him, and confirm him in his notion that there are no heroes left in the world. Before his meeting with McCarthy, over lunch at Toots Shor's, McGinniss rehearses his lines:

> What I wanted to say to him was: "Look. Once you were at the center of things. Everything revolved around you. You had squeezed your whole universe into a ball and had held it in your hands and no one could touch it. Now it's gone. The moment has passed. It won't be back." I wanted to say also that once I had been at the center of things: at twenty-six I had written a book which had become the best-selling nonfiction book in America. It had got good reviews almost everywhere. It was deemed important, and, as its author, so was I. The youngest person ever (I was told) to have written a book that became number one on the *New York Times* best-seller list. Not counting Anne Frank. Then the moment had passed. In many ways, as McCarthy had seemed to, I had tried to make it pass. Part of him had needed to not win. Part of me had needed to not succeed. . . . Now, I wanted to ask Eugene McCarthy, *What happens next? Where is the center of things? Why didn't we stay there? Will we ever be there again?*

McCarthy disappoints McGinniss by being reserved and opaque. He is "not a man inclined toward quick intimacy," McGinniss reports, and, to avoid a drinking expedition that McGinniss organizes when Howard Cosell turns up at the restaurant, McCarthy slips away while McGinniss is in the men's room. Ted Kennedy is similarly elusive. In Berrigan, McGinniss finds the expansive interlocutor he has been seeking, but the morning after their boozy late-night conversation McGinniss opens the notebook in which he inscribed Berrigan's aperçus, and instead of "the disciplined, accurate notes of a trained professional" he finds only illegible scrawls and the punch line of a coarse joke. With one striking exception, the stories McGinniss tells on himself in *Heroes* are pretty unsurprising. The exception is an extraordinary incident that takes place at ten-thirty in the morning in the kitchen of William Styron's house on Martha's Vineyard, where McGinniss has spent the night—most of it sitting up and drinking with Styron, whose book *Lie Down in Darkness* he has read four times. McGinniss writes:

I woke up at ten-thirty, if not still drunk, then not yet quite sober. The morning was murky and wet. Styron was still sleeping. I went down to the kitchen looking for something to eat. I opened the refrigerator. The first thing I saw was the can of fresh, vacuum-packed crabmeat, which had been shipped up from Georgia. He had told me about this crabmeat in some detail the night before. It was the only canned crabmeat in America, he had said, which tasted like fresh crab. This was due to the vacuum-packing, he had explained. It was very expensive crabmeat and extremely hard to get, and it was one of his favorite things to eat. He had been saving this can for a special occasion, because it was the last he would be able to get until the following summer.

I opened it. It made a hissing sound, like a can of peanuts, or tennis balls. I ate a piece. It was delicious. Moving quickly to his pantry I took out some flour. Then some Tabasco, and Worcestershire sauce. Then I took eggs, milk, heavy cream, butter, and green peppers from the refrigerator. Then I made bread crumbs. I had to move fast. I had to get this done before he woke up. I mixed, rolled, measured, stirred, and poured, for twenty minutes. Then I put the whole business in the oven. It would be crabmeat pie: an original recipe. It would be delicious. How could it miss? I had used the whole big can of crabmeat.

Styron appears in his bathrobe, and when he learns what McGinniss has done he is unbelieving, then outraged. "You used *that* crabmeat?" Styron says, and McGinniss goes on, "It was as if he had come upon me making love to his wife. 'I didn't expect you to do this,' he said." The story ends happily—Styron regains his good humor and geniality when he eats the crabmeat pie and finds it delicious—and lamely. For what the incident is about, what lies below its light surface, is the dire theme of Promethean theft, of transgression in the service of creativity, of stealing as the foundation of making. That McGinniss is rewarded, rather than punished, for his theft confuses the issue. Yes, a subject may occasionally grudgingly concede that what has been written about him isn't bad, but this doesn't make the writer any less a thief. The rare, succulent crabmeat, picked out of the shell, packed, sealed, refrigerated, jealously hoarded, is like the fragile essence of a person's being, which the journalist makes away with and turns into some horrid mess of his own while the subject sleeps. ("That crabmeat has a very delicate flavor," poor Styron whimpers on hearing of McGinniss's Tabasco and Worcestershire sauce and bread crumbs and heavy cream.) When McGinniss wrote this chapter, he could hardly have known that someday he would be in a courtroom in California having his liver ravaged by a pitiless lawyer. Or did he write those letters to MacDonald to make sure that such a fate would be his?

McGINNISS met MacDonald in June 1979, in Huntington Beach, California. McGinniss had just finished *Going to Extremes*, a work of reportage about Alaska that was to restore to him the reputation he had lost with *The*

Dream Team and *Heroes*, and establish him as a humorist of no inconsiderable gifts. He was in California as a visiting columnist for the Los Angeles *Herald Examiner*, writing a column of light, sharp commentary. However, the meeting with MacDonald put a halt to McGinniss's traffic with comedy, and brought him to a genre—the "true-crime novel"—in which he had never worked. Fortunately for him, the books of this genre published in America today apparently need to fulfill only one requirement—that they be interminably long—and when *Fatal Vision*, the true-crime novel McGinniss eventually wrote, weighed in at six hundred and sixty-three pages it insured for itself the place on the best-seller list that its publishers had anticipated when they gave him a three-hundred-thousand-dollar advance.

McGinniss was led to his subject by an item he read while scanning the Los Angeles newspapers for topics for his column: the Long Beach Police Officers Association was sponsoring a dinner dance to raise funds for the legal defense of Jeffrey MacDonald, a local physician, who was about to be tried for murder. McGinniss remembered the crime, which had occurred nine years earlier. On February 17, 1970, MacDonald's pregnant wife, Colette, aged twenty-six, and his two daughters, Kimberly and Kristen, aged five and two and a half, were bludgeoned and stabbed to death in the family's apartment at Fort Bragg, North Carolina, where MacDonald was serving as a doctor in a Green Beret unit. MacDonald was charged with the murders and then cleared by an Army tribunal. But his story about waking up to the screams of his wife and older daughter and about seeing four intruders—three men holding clubs and knives and a woman with long hair holding a candle and chanting "Acid is groovy" and "Kill the pigs"—led to no arrests, and continued to raise the question of why no traces of the intruders had been found in the apartment, and why MacDonald had been merely knocked unconscious and slightly cut up when his wife and children were savagely done to death. In response to pressure from Alfred Kassab, the stepfather of the murdered woman, the Justice Department revived the investigation in 1971 and, over a period of years, built up a compelling enough case against MacDonald to bring him to trial. In the intervening eight years, MacDonald had moved to California, and had made a life for himself that appeared to be shadowed neither by the loss of his family nor by the cloud of suspicion that had hung over him from the day of the murders. He had not remarried and was leading a pleasant, blameless life in the California style. He was a hardworking, successful physician—he had become director of emergency at St. Mary's Hospital, in Long Beach—and he lived in a small condominium apartment on the water, to which he liked to bring friends and girlfriends, often entertaining them with rides in his thirty-four-foot boat named (what else?) the *Recovery Room*. He was a handsome, tall, blond, athletic man of thirty-five, who had grown up in a lower-middle-class household in Patchogue, Long Island, the second of three children, and had always had about him a kind of preternatural equipoise, an atmosphere of being at home in the world.

MacDonald went to Princeton on a scholarship in 1961, then to Northwestern University Medical School, and then to Columbia-Presbyterian Medical Center, in New York, for his internship. In the summer following his sophomore year at Princeton and her sophomore year at Skidmore, MacDonald's girlfriend, Colette Stevenson, became pregnant. The couple decided against abortion and were married in the fall of 1963. Colette left Skidmore, and Kimberly was born in Princeton; Kristen was born in Illinois. Photographs show Colette to have been a pretty, blond girl with a soft, rounded face; all accounts of her stress her reserve, her quietness, her kindliness, and her conventional femininity. At the time of her death, she was taking an evening course in psychology at the North Carolina State University extension at Fort Bragg.

A few days before the fund-raising dinner dance, McGinniss went to see MacDonald at his apartment and interviewed him for his column. Near the end of the interview, MacDonald asked McGinniss if he would like to attend the murder trial—in Raleigh, North Carolina—and write a book about the case from the perspective of the defense team, with whom he would live, and to all of whose plans, strategies, and deliberations he would be privy. This proposal had a special appeal for McGinniss. The situation that MacDonald outlined resembled McGinniss's situation with the Nixon advertising people, which had had such a successful result. Although none of us ever completely outgrows the voyeurism of childhood, in some of us it lives on more strongly than in others—thus the avid interest of some of us in being "insiders" or in getting the "inside" view of things. In my talk with McGinniss in Williamstown, he used an arresting image: "MacDonald was clearly trying to manipulate me, and I was aware of it from the beginning. But did I have an obligation to say, 'Wait a minute. I think you are manipulating me, and I have to call your attention to the fact that I'm aware of this, just so you'll understand you are not succeeding'? Do little bells have to go off at a certain point? This has never been the case before. This could inhibit any but the most superficial reporting. We could all be reduced to standing in the street interviewing the survivors of fires."

McGinniss, of course, wanted to be in the burning house itself, and when MacDonald presented his proposition, the allure of the flames was strong enough to cause him to accept a condition that another writer might have found unacceptable—namely, that he give MacDonald a share of the book's proceeds. McGinniss was not the first writer MacDonald had approached. For many years, at the prodding of his lawyer, Bernard Segal (who had defended him before the Army tribunal, and who remained his lawyer until 1982), MacDonald had been offering himself as a subject to writers. It had been Segal's idea— fantasy, as it proved—that a book would bring in a sizable portion of the money needed to pay for MacDonald's defense. "We were running into the red substantially," Segal testified at the McGinniss trial. "People were working without salaries . . . and I thought a book with an advance that was substantial and fair would help out." Two writers who had nibbled at the bait but had not been netted were Edward Keyes and Joseph Wambaugh; Keyes couldn't get the necessary advance, and Wambaugh couldn't come to the trial, because he was making a film. The hope of finding a writer had been pretty much abandoned, and when McGinniss turned up on the eve of the trial he was like the answer to a prayer one had no longer thought worth uttering. The dovetailing of desires was remarkable: McGinniss would get his insider's spot ("I wouldn't have wanted to just go to the trial and sit out there with the other reporters," he told me. "I wanted to do it from the inside looking out, and I wanted total access to MacDonald and his lawyers"), and MacDonald would get his money.

In the deal that was presently struck—presided over by Segal and Sterling Lord, McGinniss's agent, who had got McGinniss a contract with the Dell/Delacorte publishing company and his three-hundred-thousand-dollar advance—McGinniss would receive not only total access but also a written promise of exclusivity and a release from all legal liability: MacDonald would lend himself to no other writer and would not sue McGinniss for libel if he didn't like what was written. For his part, MacDonald would receive twenty-six and a half per cent of the advance and thirty-three per cent of the royalties. The arrangement was a kind of reification of the hopes and good intentions that writers and subjects normally exchange at the beginning of their enterprise. The money that MacDonald was to get was simply a more tangible manifestation of the reward that every subject expects to receive at the end of the project—why else would he lend himself to it? And, similarly, the written assurances that McGinniss received from MacDonald were no different from the tacit ones that writers normally receive from subjects: It is *understood* that the subject will not sue, and that he will not faithlessly go to another writer.

It is understood—and yet it is also known that subjects do sometimes sue writers, and that they do sometimes leave one writer for another, or abruptly break off the interviews. It is the latter eventuality, with its immediate disastrous effect on his project, that causes the writer the greatest anxiety (a lawsuit can occur only after the project is completed, in some hazy distant future) and impels him toward the devices and disingenuousnesses that came under such unprecedentedly close scrutiny in the MacDonald-McGinniss lawsuit. But the writer isn't alone in his anxiety. Even as he is worriedly striving to keep the subject talking, the subject is worriedly striving to keep the writer *listening*. The subject is Scheherazade. He lives in fear of being found uninteresting, and many of the strange things that subjects say to writers—things of almost suicidal rashness—they say out of their desperate need to keep the writer's attention riveted. In the MacDonald-McGinniss encounter—the encounter of a man accused of a terrible crime with a journalist whom he tries to keep listening to his tale of innocence—we have a grotesquely magnified version of the normal journalistic encounter. Even though the crimes to which the normal subject pleads innocent—vanity, hypocrisy, pomposity, inanity, mediocrity—are less serious than those of which MacDonald stood accused, the outcome tends to be the same: as MacDonald's tale ultimately failed to hold McGinniss—whose attention soon shifted to the rhetorically superior story of the prosecution—so do the majority of stories told to journalists fail of their object. The writer ultimately tires of the subject's self-serving story, and substitutes a story of his own. The story of subject and writer is the Scheherazade story with a bad ending: in almost no case does the subject manage to, as it were, save himself.

As if sensing the deeper structures of the Devil's pact he was brokering between MacDonald and McGinniss, Segal, when called upon to approve a release from McGinniss's publisher, scribbled in a proviso whose language, on first reading, seems oddly ambiguous for a lawyer to use. The release was dated August 3, 1979, and was written in the form of a letter from MacDonald to McGinniss which began, "I understand you are writing a book about my life centering on my current trial for murder." The letter's third paragraph, where Segal's emendation took place, originally read:

> I realize, of course, that you do not propose to libel me. Nevertheless, in order that you may feel free to write the book in any manner that you may deem best, I agree that I will not make or assert against you, the publisher, or its licensees or anyone else involved in the production or distribution of the book, any claim or demand whatsoever based on the ground that anything contained in the book defames me.

Segal felt constrained to change the final period to a comma and to add these words: "provided that the essential integrity of my life story is maintained." Eight years later, in the MacDonald-McGinniss suit, it became MacDonald's contention that the "essential integrity" of his life story had not been maintained in McGinniss's book, and that McGinniss was guilty of a kind of soul murder, for which it was necessary that he be brought to account. The federal judge assigned to the case, William Rea, also seemed to hear the Commendatore's music wafting out of the complaint and, in his denial of McGinniss's motion for summary judgment, to concur with the plaintiff's moralistic view of the case.

But all this was many years into the future. In the summer of 1979, MacDonald and McGinniss were Damon and Pythias. In common with many other subjects and writers, they clothed their complicated business together in the mantle of friendship—in this case, friendship of a particularly American cast, whose emblems of intimacy are watching sports on television, drinking beer, running, and classifying women according to looks. A few weeks after writing about MacDonald for the *Herald Examiner*, McGinniss gave up his guest column and flew to Raleigh to take up his insider's post with the MacDonald defense; he moved into the Kappa Alpha fraternity house on the North Carolina State University campus, which Segal had rented for the summer, and there joined MacDonald, his mother, Segal, and the various lawyers, paralegals, law students, and volunteers of the defense group. One member of this group was Michael Malley, a lawyer, who had been MacDonald's roommate at Princeton and had taken part in MacDonald's defense at the Army hearing that dismissed the charges against him in 1970. Now, on leave from his law firm in Phoenix, Malley had once again put himself at the service of his friend, and, alone of the group, was not happy about the insertion of McGinniss into its midst. As Malley was to testify later, he had nothing against McGinniss personally—indeed, he liked him, as everyone else did—but he felt there was something fundamentally risky about letting a writer into the inner councils of the defense. "I felt that if Joe was there all the time, we had a real problem about the attorney-client privilege," Malley said, adding, by way of explanation, "The privilege is that anything you say to your attorney isn't going to go beyond the attorney unless the client agrees to it. But if there is an outsider present, somebody who doesn't belong to the defense team, the privilege is waived. And Joe, to me, clearly seemed to be an outsider, and I simply didn't like it." Malley told Segal of his concern about McGinniss, and Segal came up with a solution to the problem of the attorney-client privilege which Malley reluctantly accepted: McGinniss would be made an official member of the defense team—he would sign an employment agreement with Segal—and would thus be protected against, for example, any attempt by the prosecution to get at the defense's secrets by subpoenaing his notes.

The criminal trial in Raleigh lasted seven weeks and ended, on August 29, with MacDonald's conviction—to the shock and horror of the defense. McGinniss, on hearing the verdict, cried, as did everyone else in the defense group. MacDonald was put in handcuffs and taken to a federal prison in Butner, North Carolina. The next day, he wrote a letter to McGinniss—the first letter in a correspondence that was to last almost four years. "I've got to write to you so I won't go crazy," he began. His letter ended with this emotional paragraph:

> I want to see Bernie [Segal], because I love him & he is probably hurting beyond belief & wants to know he is not to blame. I want to see my Mom, because no matter how I look, by seeing me she will be better (and I probably will be, too). I would also love to see my best friends— including (I hope) you. But in all honesty, I'm crying too much today, and do cry whenever I think of my close friends. I feel dirty & soiled by the decision & can't tell you why, and am ashamed. I somehow don't feel that way with Bernie & Mom but think today it would be difficult to look at you or shake your hand—I know I'll cry and want to hug you—and yet the verdict stands there, screaming, "You are guilty of the murder of your family!!" And I don't know what to say to you except it is not true, and I hope you know that and feel it and that you are my friend.

McGinniss did not "know that." In the course of the trial, he had become persuaded of MacDonald's guilt and had found himself once again in the position—the one he had held with the Nixon advertising group—of enemy infiltrator. In July 1983, two months before the publication of *Fatal Vision*, Bob Keeler, a reporter from *Newsday*, who had also attended the criminal trial, interviewed McGinniss for an article he was writing for *The Newsday Magazine* and questioned him closely about the uncomfortableness of his situation in Raleigh. "There was nobody to talk to," McGinniss told Keeler. "I couldn't react. I couldn't say to someone sitting next to me in the courtroom, 'Hey, this doesn't sound good.' "

"What was your anticipation of the result when the jury went out to deliberate?" Keeler asked.

"I was not convinced they were going to convict him. At the same time, I said to myself, 'If I were a juror I would vote to convict.' But I didn't think that those twelve people were all going to come to the same conclusion I had come to. I didn't know if it was going to be a hung jury or an acquittal. But I think I would have predicted either of those two results ahead of the conviction."

"O.K. So the day after the conviction you went down to Butner, and Jeff hugs you and says he hopes you're going to be his friend forever. What were your feelings at the moment? Obviously, by that time you must have known the book was going to come out showing him to be a guilty guy. How did you feel at that moment?"

"I felt terribly conflicted. I knew he had done it—no question—but I had just spent the summer with the guy, who on one level is a terribly easy person to like. But how can you like a guy who has killed his wife and kids? It was a very complex set of emotions I felt, and I was very happy to leave him behind in prison."

Later in the interview, Keeler asked McGinniss this blunt question: "One of the theories among the reporters at the trial was that you were going to write this Jeffrey MacDonald-the-tortured-innocent book. Another theory was that you were going to do to Jeffrey MacDonald what you'd done to Richard M. Nixon—that is to say, to be in his presence and in his confidence for a number of months and then run it up his butt sideways. And I'm wondering, since the latter has turned out to be the case, whether that's going to provide a problem for you in the future. That is to say, is anybody ever going to trust you again?"

"Well, they can trust me if they're innocent," McGinniss retorted.

"You don't feel that you in any sense betrayed Jeffrey or did him dirt or anything?"

"My only obligation from the beginning was to the truth."

"How would you describe your feelings about Jeffrey MacDonald now? This is a complex question, obviously, but obviously you're going to be asked this on talk shows, and you're going to have thirty seconds or ten seconds to think about it. How would you describe it?"

"Right now, I have a strange absence of feeling toward him. He has occupied so much of my consciousness and subconscious for so long that, with the book finally done, I find myself kind of numb in regard to him. I don't have a feeling except the feeling that has been with me, which isn't focussed so specifically on him but on the whole thing—a sadness that just doesn't go away. It's just sadness, sadness, sadness. Such a tragic, terrible waste, and such a dark and internally persecuted human being he is. He is so different from what he appears to be. I feel very sad that he didn't turn out to be who he wanted me to think he was. Because that would have been a lot easier to handle."

MacDONALD was transferred from the Butner prison to the Terminal Island Federal Correctional Institution, near Long Beach, California—after a bus trip that spread over several weeks, during which he was kept in shackles—and in November McGinniss flew out to see him there and to continue his research for the book. Although he had glued himself to MacDonald in North Carolina, McGinniss had put off interviewing him about his life before the murders until the trial was over; now he would do this work. But at the prison McGinniss was prevented from bringing a tape recorder, or even a notebook and pencil, into the visiting room. So the men devised a scheme that would take the place of interviews: MacDonald would recollect his past into a tape recorder and mail the tapes (via his mother) to McGinniss. Over the next two years, MacDonald sent McGinniss a total of thirty tapes, which he made under somewhat mysterious circumstances (How did he get a tape recorder into his cell? Why was he never caught recording? Why was the tape recorder never found by guards? Why was his mother never caught smuggling the tapes out?), and from which McGinniss quoted excerpts in his book in chapters entitled "The Voice of Jeffrey MacDonald," alternating with the narrative proper. McGinniss stayed in California a week, and during his stay MacDonald put his empty condominium—a half hour's drive from the prison—at McGinniss's disposal. McGinniss slept in a guest room–office, and during the day (he visited MacDonald in the late afternoon) he would read in the massive files on the case that MacDonald kept there and had given him carte blanche to rifle. McGinniss found so much of interest in the files that he asked MacDonald if he might take some of the material back home with him; the ever-obliging Mac-Donald agreed, and even lent him a suitcase in which to cart the stuff. Among the documents McGinniss found in the apartment, the most exciting to him was an account MacDonald had handwritten for his attorneys at the Army hearing in 1970. In it (the document was later made public), he listed all his activities on the evening of the murders and mentioned a diet pill, Eskatrol—an amphetamine combined with a sedative—that he had been taking. McGinniss, baffled, like everyone else, as to what could have prompted MacDonald to kill his family, and in such a savage way, consulted various pharmaceutical texts and found that Eskatrol could induce psychosis when taken in high enough doses. (It was removed from the market in 1980.) MacDonald had written:

> We ate dinner together at 5:45 p.m. (all four). It is possible I had one diet pill at this time. I do not remember, and do not think I had one, but it is possible. I had been running a weight-control program for my unit, and I put my name at the top of the program to encourage participation. I had lost 12–15 lbs. in the prior 3–4 weeks, in the process using 3–5 capsules of Eskatrol Spansule. [Quoting this passage in *Fatal Vision*, McGinniss dropped the clause "and do not think I had one."]

Not implausibly, McGinniss interpreted "3–5 capsules" to mean three to five capsules a *day*, which is an overdose, and he went on to propose in *Fatal Vision* that MacDonald killed his wife and daughters in a fit of rage—a rage against the female sex that he had been repressing since early childhood and that the drug (in combination with stress, fatigue, and Colette MacDonald's threatening "new insights into personality structure and behavioral patterns," picked up at the psychology course she was taking and had just come home from) finally permitted him to vent. McGinniss based his theory of the crime on an uncritical reading of three moral tracts—Otto Kernberg's *Borderline Conditions and Pathological Narcissism*, Christopher Lasch's *The Culture of Narcissism*, and Hervey Cleckley's *The Mask of Sanity*—in which the terms "psychopath" and "pathological narcissist" are confidently offered as the answer to the problem of evil (as if labelling were ever anything more than the restatement of a problem). In the MacDonald-McGinniss trial, to lend credence to McGinniss's labelling of MacDonald as a pathological narcissist, Kornstein invited Kernberg himself to appear as an expert witness and apply to MacDonald the adjectives he applies to the patients in his book—"grandiose," "cold," "shallow," "ruthless," "exploitative," "parasitic," "haughty," "envious," "self-centered," "lacking in emotional depth," "deficient in genuine feelings of sadness"—who suffer from the malady he has invented. Kernberg prudently declined, and suggested a colleague of his, Michael Stone, for the role of moralist-in-shrink's-clothing, which Stone accepted and played to the hilt.

Another arresting find of McGinniss's at the MacDonald apartment was a letter from Joseph Wambaugh, dated March 28, 1975, spelling out the conditions under which he would consider writing a book about MacDonald. The letter's tone is more like that of the charmless writing in small print on a baggage-claim check than like the communication of an author to a prospective subject. As he read, McGinniss must have marvelled at, and possibly envied, Wambaugh's *je m'en foutisme*. But then Wambaugh was an ex-cop (he was once a detective on the Los Angeles police force), and, maybe even more to the point, he was one of America's most successful popular writers, who apparently could afford to be blunt (as McGinniss, strapped for cash, apparently could not). "You should understand that I would not think of writing *your* story," Wambaugh wrote, and he went on:

> It would be *my* story. Just as *The Onion Field* was *my* story and *In Cold Blood* was Capote's story. We both had the living persons sign legal releases which authorized us to interpret, portray, and characterize them as we saw fit, trusting us implicitly to be honest and faithful to the truth as *we* saw it, not as *they* saw it.
>
> With this release you can readily see that you would have no recourse at law if you didn't like my portrayal of you. Let's face another ugly possibility: what if I, after spending months of research and interviewing dozens of people and listening to hours of court trials, did not believe you innocent?
>
> I suspect that you may want a writer who would tell *your* story, and indeed your version may very well be the truth as I would see it. But you'd have *no* guarantee, not with me. You'd have absolutely *no* editorial prerogative. You would not even see the book until publication.

McGinniss quotes this letter in *Fatal Vision*, and also quotes from a note that MacDonald sent to Segal about the letter: "What do you think? He sounds awfully arrogant to me, but it will be an obvious best-seller if he writes the book." McGinniss goes on, "Wambaugh, of course, had not written the book. . . . Now I was writing it." He adds, assuming some of Wambaugh's toughness, "As would have been the case with Wambaugh, MacDonald had absolutely no editorial prerogative. And the 'ugly possibility' to which Wambaugh referred had now become a reality."

But toward MacDonald himself McGinniss continued to behave with his customary ingratiation. For almost four years—during which he corresponded with MacDonald, spoke with him on the telephone, received his tapes, and, on two occasions, visited him—he successfully hid the fact that in the book under preparation he was portraying MacDonald as a psychopathic killer. In 1981, writing to his editor at Dell, Morgan Entrekan, about the book's narrative strategy, he expressed his concern lest its protagonist seem "too loathsome too soon," and proposed that the worst revelations about his character be "postponed until the end, when we draw closer and closer to him, seeing the layers of the mask melt away and gazing, at least obliquely, at the essence of the horror which lurks beneath." He added—referring to his uneasy relations with the actual MacDonald—"The ice is getting thinner, and I'm still a long way from shore." But he need not have worried; MacDonald never twigged to the ruse. Like the dupe in the Milgram deception, the naïve subject of a book becomes so caught up in the enterprise and so emotionally invested in it that he simply cannot conceive of it in any terms other than those the writer has set for it. As the Milgram subject imagined he was "helping" someone to learn, so MacDonald imagined he was "helping" McGinniss write a book exonerating him of the crime, and presenting him as a kind of kitsch hero ("loving father and husband," "dedicated physician," "overachiever"). When, instead, McGinniss wrote a book charging him with the crime, and presenting him as a kitsch villain ("publicity-seeker," "womanizer," "latent homosexual"), MacDonald was stunned. His dehoaxing took place in a particularly dramatic and cruel manner. McGinniss had steadfastly refused to let him see galleys or an advance copy of the book. In a letter of February 16, 1983, he had written sternly, "I understand your impatience, and it is to that that I will attribute the unpleasantness of your tone. . . . At no time was there ever any understanding that you would be given an advance look at the book six months prior to publication. As Joe Wambaugh told you in 1975, with him you would not even see a copy before it was published. Same with me. Same with any principled and responsible author." MacDonald had accepted the rebuke, and had enthusiastically lent himself to the pre-publication publicity campaign for the book. His assignment was an appearance on the television show "60 Minutes," and it was during the taping of the show in prison that the fact of McGinniss's duplicity was brought home to him. As Mike Wallace—who had received an advance copy of *Fatal Vision* without difficulty or a lecture—read out loud to MacDonald passages in which he was portrayed as a psychopathic killer, the camera recorded his look of shock and utter discomposure.

Milgram, in the chapter on methodology in *Obedience to Authority*, explains that he did not use Yale undergraduates as subjects because of the risk that word of the experiment might get out among the student population. But there is reason to think—extrapolating from the writer-subject experiment—that even subjects who had heard of the Milgram experiment would have fallen into its trap after only a slight alteration of its character. MacDonald, after all, had heard of people who were displeased with what was written about them (sometimes to the point of suing the writer), and still he behaved as if there were no possibility that his "own" book could be anything but flattering and gratifying. Perhaps even more striking is MacDonald's continuing and, under the circumstances, crazy trust in the good intentions of journalists. To this day, after all that has happened to him, he continues to give interviews to journalists, continues to correspond with them, continues to send them material (through an out-of-prison information office run by a woman named Gail Boyce), and does everything he can to be helpful to them, just as he did with McGinniss. Something seems to happen to people when they meet a journalist, and what happens is exactly the opposite of what one would expect. One would think that extreme wariness and caution would be the order of the day, but in fact childish trust and impetuosity are far more common. The journalistic encounter seems to have the same regressive effect on a subject as the psychoanalytic encounter. The subject becomes a kind of child of the writer, regarding him as a permissive, all-accepting, all-forgiving mother, and expecting that the book will be written by her. Of course, the book is written by the strict, all-noticing, unforgiving father. During our conversation in Williamstown, McGinniss quoted the following passage from an essay by Thomas Mann, which he had come upon in a book by another of his literary heroes, Joseph Campbell:

> The look that one directs at things, both outward and inward, as an artist, is not the same as that with which one would regard the same as a man, but at once colder and more passionate. As a man, you might be well-disposed, patient, loving, positive, and have a wholly uncritical inclination to look upon everything as all right, but as artist your daemon constrains you to "observe," to take note,

lightning fast and with hurtful malice, of every detail that in the literary sense would be characteristic, distinctive, significant, opening insights, typifying the race, the social or the psychological mode, recording all as mercilessly as though you had no human relationship to the observed object whatever.

"This isn't something that you can argue before a jury of people who don't read books," McGinniss said to me, "but it seems to me to get right to the heart of it." He told me that he had "compartmentalized" his conflicting attitudes toward MacDonald. "The first letter I got from the guy, written eighteen hours after his conviction, brought tears to my eyes. I felt genuine sorrow. He wrote, 'All I want to know is that you're still my friend and you believe in me.' So what's the appropriate response? To send back a paragraph that says, 'I reserve the right to my own opinions, and I remind you that I'm the author and you are the subject, and we have to keep things on that level'? Or do I write back and say, 'You sound terrible, prison must be awful, I really feel bad for you'? All of which was an expression of genuine feeling at that time on my part. Not a lie. But I was compartmentalizing. I was suspending my critical faculty long enough to allow me to write that letter."

The letter in question was written on September 11, 1979, twelve days after MacDonald's first letter to McGinniss. It read, in part:

Dear Jeff,

Every morning for a week now, I've been waking up wondering where you are. A bus! Christ! It seems that the only function a ride across country in a prison bus might serve is to make your destination seem not quite as awful as it otherwise would have. On the other hand, I'm sure your destination seems awful. Is awful. Terminal Island. Pretty terrible name, on top of everything else. . . .

I am glad to see that you are able to write—to describe and analyze both what happened to you and your own feelings about it. I have plenty of my own thoughts, which I'll be getting to sooner or later, but mostly I am relieved to see that you are apparently able to function constructively despite the extreme limitations. Also, I'm glad you didn't kill yourself, because that sure would have been a bummer for the book. . . .

There could not be a worse nightmare than the one you are living through now—but it is only a phase. Total strangers can recognize within five minutes that you did not receive a fair trial. . . .

Well, I'm sure when I see you we will have plenty of chance to talk about that as well as many other things. Bob Keeler, incidentally, told me he planned to spend quite a bit of time interviewing you at Terminal Island. Told me also he wants to write a book on the case & is talking to Doubleday about it. I would just as soon he did not write a book; & Delacorte will be announcing my book—and the full and exclusive access aspect of our relationship—this week to try and keep the field reasonably clear. Frankly, I am not sure what Keeler's attitude toward you is. I'm not implying that he believes you are guilty—I just don't know, but I think it would be better on many counts if you did nothing to encourage or to assist anyone else who might be planning to write about this. . . .

You must fear—on top of everything else—that you will somehow become a non-person. Just—poof—there is no more Jeff. There is just this big empty space where he was. Well, that's not going to happen, because there are too many people who care too much about you, and please try to remember that during those hours and days when you feel at your worst. . . . I will be back home by Sept. 25—into N.Y. on Sept. 26 for meetings about this book with Delacorte—it's a dinner, actually, where the president of the company & Sterling [Lord] & I will try to block out a reasonable timetable & where I explain to them how things managed to take this drastic & unexpected turn for the shitty. . . . I have much, much more to say, but I do want you to receive at least this much from me by the time you reach Cal. . . . I'll write again in a couple of days. Jeff, it's all so fucking awful I can't believe it yet—the sight of the jury coming in—of the jury polling—of you standing—saying those few words—being led out—and then seeing you in a fucking prison. It's a hell of a thing—spend the summer making a new friend and then the bastards come along and lock him up. But not for long, Jeffrey—not for long.

More soon—
Joe

On September 28, 1979, McGinniss wrote again:

. . . I am very relieved that you are at last in a place where they do not keep you in shackles all day. . . . I am hoping that you won't even be there very long; that the folks in Richmond [the federal appeals court] recognize and act upon the validity of the bail appeal. . . .

What I propose is to fly to California, prepared to stay for a while. To see you, as much as possible, either at this location where fate and bureaucracy have combined to put you, or, far better for both of us, in Huntington Beach. In any event, that is when our real work can begin. Aside from the money, and the fact that someday the full story will be told, it seems to me that one very important benefit of the book is that it gives you something constructive to do day by day. Something real; something valuable; something essential. A way to channel your anger and reflections. A book about the case; no convict should be without one. (Even in jest, it doesn't feel right to type the word "convict" in reference to you, and I am hoping like hell this phase will come to as quick and merciful a halt as possible next week in Richmond with the granting of bail. . . .

Jeff, it is still very hard to accept all of this. To have you writing about prison and life on the bus. To be trying to answer all the questions about what went wrong: the most obvious answers, of course, are the ones you've already come up with. Jury selection. It was utter madness . . . was, all by itself, probably all the answer anyone would ever need as to what went wrong. . . .

Goddamn, Jeff, one of the worst things about all this is how suddenly and totally all your friends—self included—have been deprived of the pleasure of your company. . . . What the fuck were those people thinking of? How could 12 people not only agree to believe such a horrendous proposition, but agree, with a man's life at stake, that they believed it beyond a reasonable doubt? In six and a half hours? . . .

As you have no doubt gathered, I do not devote the care to word selection and organization in my letters that I do in my books. Generally, I don't write letters at all. One of the reasons my phone bill each month is almost as high as the mortgage. Writing, for me, is work, and I do not like to do my work carelessly, but if I waited until I got a letter into the shape I'd be happy with, you would never hear another word from me and would think I had perished on a mountain or had instead undertaken to write the life story of Freddy Kassab. So, even as imperfectly as I have expressed it, what I mean is I am still sorry as hell this whole thing ever happened, and am impatient to see you again and to plunge into the book, and, hopefully, once again to share with you many laughs and good stories and new experiences as well as re-living, in sorrow, some of the bad ones from the past. . . .

These early letters, like the overture to an opera, announce all the themes of the coming correspondence. Until close to the publication of *Fatal Vision*, when McGinniss apparently felt he could afford to be a bit cold and careless with MacDonald, he wrote letters assuring MacDonald of his friendship, commiserating with him about his situation, offering him advice about his appeal, requesting information for the book, and fretting about competing writers. The passages dealing with this last concern—a very common one among writers (every writer thinks someone else is working on his subject; it is part of the paranoid state of mind necessary for the completion of the infinitely postponable task of writing)—make especially painful reading, in a correspondence full of painful moments. McGinniss had a real cause for worry: two people were actually planning to write books about the MacDonald case. One was Bob Keeler, who had been covering the case for *Newsday* since the early seventies; the other was Freddy Kassab, the stepfather of the murdered woman, who was looking for an as-told-to writer to set forth his version. But the measures that McGinniss, his agent, and his publisher took to insure that no one but McGinniss would come out with a book about MacDonald were extraordinarily active. In the letter of September 28, McGinniss also wrote:

I mentioned to your Mom last night that I felt strongly you should not start doing a bunch of interviews while in prison. There's no way that kind of thing can do you any good right now; I am thinking of Keeler in particular. Whether or not he is going ahead with his book I do not know, but, frankly, the one and only one in which you have any interest is the one to which I will be devoting the next two years of my life. . . . Sterling and Ross Claiborne [vice-president of Dell], incidentally, both felt very strongly that any major stories, interviews, etc. done with you at this time would undermine my position to some extent.

Then, on November 19, 1979, McGinniss to MacDonald:

Keeler seems awfully plugged in, & your Mom says he's been nosing around Schenectady & vicinity trying to get old acquaintances of your sister's to talk. Sounds to me like he is definitely doing a book, and with Freddy still trying to do his own, you & I had better get asses in gear.

McGinniss to MacDonald, December 18, 1979:

Freddy Kassab has made it official. The New York Times book division . . . has given him a contract for a book about you and the murders and how he eventually brought you to trial. . . . The first thing this means is that now Freddy will never talk to me about anything, which will make certain aspects of my book a little more complicated, and the second thing is I want to be sure that the two books are not published at the same time, or even in the same season. I really don't care which comes first: I just don't want them coming out together. Can you imagine me going around the country on talk shows with that guy?

I wonder whether from your end, it might not be a good idea to have Bernie [Segal] send some sort of letter to New York Times Books and/or to the writer, reminding them of the extent to which libel and invasion of privacy laws might apply in this situation. . . .

Anyway, New York Times Books is not, despite the impressiveness of anything with NY Times in the title, a particularly attractive place to wind up. It is most certainly not in the first, or even second echelon of publishers, but even so, your personal life and my professional life would both be a bit simpler if Freddy Kassab were not writing his own book. If a timely reminder of legal implications might still be able to forestall this, I would think it worth a try. . . .

Just as I wrote that, I decided to call Ross Claiborne back and see what he thought of all this. First, he tells me he has just received another call, this time from an editor at Time-Life books, saying they were "considering" a proposal for "a book" about MacDonald, etc. This editor wanted to know the status of mine, and Ross C. said, oh, it's very far along; research completed; writing is coming very well; he's well into it. This is known in the trade as heading off at the pass. The Time-Life editor did not say whose proposal they were considering, and now the situation is extremely confused. Is this a third book in the offing (possibly by Keeler?). Or, is *this* the Freddy proposal, still not accepted, but only being considered by Time-Life, and not the NY Times? . . . It may be tomorrow, actually, before I hear back on any of this, but, at any rate, you're getting a rare inside glimpse into the wonderful world of publishing and how sometimes gamesmanship can be almost as much of a factor as literary merit.

McGinniss to MacDonald, December 20, 1979:

Update from the ever-changing publishing world: the New York Times Books is not, repeat not, doing a Freddy Kassab book. Ross Claiborne's original info was wrong. . . .

In early January Delacorte/Dell will issue a release to *Publishers Weekly*, *Variety*, and other interested outlets that they have *this* book in the works, and it's a big deal, and etc. etc. to try to drive away any other interested bystanders. That sort of thing also generates some movie interest as well.

McGinniss to MacDonald, January 10, 1980:

Keeler's opus will run in *Newsday* sometime soon, and he probably plans to use that as his book proposal—showing how much work he's already done—so, to try and defuse this whole scene a little bit, Delacorte/Dell as of this morning is issuing a flashy news release, to be sent to all the usual media outlets . . . saying that big-name author (me) has been signed to six-figure contract to do big deal book on most bizarre crime story of the decade; that sort of thing. They are emphasizing my "total and exclusive" access to you, as well as how far along the whole project already is; making it sound, actually, as if the book is two-thirds written. . . . Sterling is checking this week with some sources at *Newsday* to try to find out for me when Keeler's piece will run. Sounds like it will be quite a big deal. I am uncomfortable thinking that someone else already knows more about any aspect of this than I do, but Keeler obviously is way ahead of me in Patchogue. I trust we'll be able to catch up. You can see, though, the wisdom in not cooperating with him.

McGinniss to MacDonald, February 26, 1980:

Keeler's thing came out last weekend, and it sure was a piece of crap. Whew! Real cheap soap-opera shit. Not overtly hostile to you—particularly considering his personal feelings—but just such a shitty piece of work. Badly written—atrociously written, in fact, which surprised me, because his basic trial coverage was well done—sloppily organized, and just, in the end, pointless. . . . Makes me wonder what the value would be of all Keeler's six years of research stuff from Long Island.

McGinniss to MacDonald, March 18, 1980:

I get back here to discover, through a somewhat frantic phone call from Ross Claiborne, that Freddy has apparently succeeded in getting a publisher for his book, and, what is more troubling, has obtained the services of a first-rate writer to do the book. The writer's name is J. D. Reed, and he is on the staff of *Sports Illustrated* but also the author of "Free Fall," a novel about the D. B. Cooper caper, which is selling very well and has just been bought for a movie, giving Reed a temporarily hot hand, and apparently causing great Hollywood interest in the Freddy story as a movie.

McGinniss to MacDonald, March 28, 1980:

Update from the land of eastern standard time, big-time publishing, and gray, post-winter days that don't know when to quit. . . .

I talked to Bernie last weekend and he said he would send letters both to the president of Doubleday and Reed. . . . Reed has already told Ross Claiborne he is "not committed" to this project and that, in the light of all this, he would certainly have to give it a whole new look. I've heard nothing since then, but I can guarantee you that a letter from Bernie to Doubleday will make them take a very close look at the project, and with both author and publisher wavering, Freddy could find himself heading back to square one. We shall see. . . .

GARY BOSTWICK is a forty-nine-year-old man of unexceptional appearance—he is plump, wears a shaggy mustache, and has small eyes behind wire-frame glasses—who immediately strikes one as a man of exceptional decency, good humor, and quickness of mind. If McGinniss's chief problem as defendant was his letters to MacDonald, a close second in bad breaks was the drawing of Bostwick as opposing counsel. "I love juries," Bostwick often says. More to the point, juries love him. Jurors sit there presumably weighing evidence but in actuality they are studying character. They miss little. When I spoke to the jurors of the MacDonald-McGinniss case and asked them their impressions of the two lawyers, they offered a low opinion of Kornstein, derived in large part from the way he frequently humiliated a young associate; in one instance, the associate made what Kornstein perceived as a mistake while examining a witness, and Kornstein peremptorily ordered him to sit down. Bostwick's behavior, in contrast, had been impeccable, the jurors reported. A question that was asked by many people during the trial and after was: How could such a good man have taken on such a terrible client—a client who had murdered his wife and children and now had the gall to sue a reputable author for writing a book about him that he didn't like? This was the sort of case, it was felt, that would attract the lowest sort of contingency-fee hustler, not an attorney of probity and reputation. Although Bostwick—who was not working on a contingency basis but at his regular rates—was never able to change this view of the case as it was reflected in the newspapers, on the radio, and on television, he succeeded in causing five (out of the six) jurors and an alternate to accept his version of the MacDonald-McGinniss encounter as a sort of Conradian fable of moral failure, and of the trial as a necessary ritual of retribution.

On the face of it, one would have thought that Bostwick's task was extremely difficult, if not impossible. It is one thing to call Lord Jim to account for his betrayal of the trust of the innocent pilgrims aboard his ship, and another to try a journalist for his sins against a man convicted of a crime so horrible that it renders the journalist's sins innocuous in comparison. But among the many curiosities and surprises of this curious and surprising lawsuit was the ease with which Bostwick was able to make his case, and the difficulty that Kornstein had with his. As Kornstein must have been dismayed to learn, having a murderer for your adversary does not give you an automatic advantage. Kornstein's strategy of constantly reminding the jury of MacDonald's conviction did not serve him well. The jurors said they held this against him, feeling it an insult to their intelligence. (They were nudged toward this reaction by Bostwick, who, in his final argument, compared Kornstein's constant references to MacDonald as "the convicted murderer" to a detergent commercial in which the word "Oxydol was mentioned twenty-seven times in three minutes, so that people would not forget that Oxydol was the thing to buy.")

But there may be a deeper reason for the jurors' almost bovine equanimity in the face of MacDonald's crime. This reason can be stated as a corollary to society's need to punish the transgressor, which is the need to forgive the transgressor. The crime of murder is one we have all committed in our (conscious and unconscious) imaginations. We have all dreamed about the violent deaths of our families; we have all said about people we love "I could kill him" (or her). In our old literature, we have Medea, Clytemnestra, and Oedipus acting out these fundamental fantasies; more recently, and thus more veiledly, we have Raskolnikov killing his mother and his sister through the murder of two strangers. And as we need to be punished and then absolved of our guilt, so do we punish and then absolve those who actually do what we only dream of doing. One of the unsolved mysteries of the case was McGinniss's preternatural hardness toward MacDonald both in his book and in the statements he made to the press after its publication. As the trial went on, it was this hardness—McGinniss's apparent incapacity for feeling compassion for MacDonald—rather than MacDonald's crime, that came to seem monstrous to the jurors. One of them, a young black woman named Sheila Campbell, articulated this feeling to me. "The part I didn't like was when MacDonald let McGinniss use his condominium, and McGinniss took it upon himself to find the motive for the murders," she said. "I didn't like the fact that McGinniss tried to find a motive for a book that was a best-seller, and that's *all* he was concerned about. He wasn't concerned about MacDonald as a human being whatsoever. He said he had feelings for Colette and the kids. But when are you going to start forgiving someone even if they did commit the crime? Are you going to torture the man for the rest of his life?"

MacDonald's own appearance at the trial did nothing to dissuade anyone from thinking of him as a person worthy of forgiveness. Dressed in a subdued business suit, he sat quietly at the plaintiff's table, and the association of this sobersided man with the straight-arrow Bostwick gave the jurors further permission to regard MacDonald's crime and punishment as a closed book, and to see him as a kind of nearly, if not fully, redeemed soul, who had suffered, whom it was not their place to judge, and whose punishment by McGinniss had been excessive and unfair.

Bostwick's punishment of McGinniss, on the other hand—his relentless and pitiless interrogation—seemed neither excessive nor unfair to the jurors, they reported, nor inconsistent with his persona as a good man. With the flaming sword he had been handed in the form of McGinniss's letters, he had no trouble playing the role of avenging angel. "It is a case about a false friend," he dramatically announced in his opening statement. What he did not articulate to the jurors but what a reader of the transcript cannot help noting is the (in this case) ironic parallel between the methods of trial lawyers and of journalists. The devastating narrative that Bostwick spun out of McGinniss's heedless epistolary chatter was like the narrative that a journalist spins out of a subject's careless talk during an interview. As the subject blathers on and on, apparently oblivious of the notebook or tape recorder that is catching the words on which he is later to be impaled, so McGinniss was apparently oblivious of the consequences of leaving behind a written record of his intimacy with MacDonald, with whom he evidently felt so comfortable that he could confide in him his secrets from "the wonderful world of publishing"—like a businessman confiding the details of the day's deals to a trusted mistress. And just as the subject, after the book or article comes out, will desperately attempt to unsay the things he wishes he had not said to the journalist, so, at the trial, did McGinniss attempt to repudiate his letters to MacDonald.

" 'What the fuck were those people thinking of? How could twelve people not only agree to believe such a horrendous proposition but agree, with a man's life at stake, that they believed it beyond a reasonable doubt in six and a half hours?' " Bostwick read aloud from McGinniss's second letter to MacDonald. He then turned to McGinniss and said, "Did you believe that when you wrote it to him?" McGinniss replied, "I did and I still do. I think it's the most horrendous proposition in the world that a man could murder his wife and two little girls." The transcript continues:

> Q: What I'm asking you, Mr. McGinniss, is something else. Didn't you try to tell him with those words that you found it hard to believe that the jury had come to the verdict they did?
>
> A: I was surprised it only took them six and a half hours, but my perspective, you'll have to remember, was totally and entirely from one side during that trial. I spent my time only with MacDonald, not with the prosecution.
>
> Q: I understand that, Mr. McGinniss. What I'm asking you is whether you were trying to get Dr. MacDonald to believe that you believed the jury had been wrong.
>
> A: No.
>
> Q: You weren't, not with those words?
>
> A: I didn't feel that the jury—
>
> Q: I'm just asking you what you were trying to get Dr. MacDonald to believe with those words.
>
> A: I have no recollection of what I was trying to get Dr. MacDonald to believe.

Bostwick continued to tighten the screws: "Did you consider yourself [MacDonald's] friend at the end of trial?"

> A: I considered myself the author, I considered him the subject during those six or seven weeks. We certainly got along well. I don't know how you define "friend." It was a professional relationship.

Q: How do *you* define "friend"?

A: I defined "friend" as someone whose company I enjoy from time to time; someone whose—with whom I would have reason to stay in some kind of contact. I have never really stopped and thought about a definition of the word "friend," but I'm sure we could find one in a dictionary. But Dr. MacDonald was the subject, and I was the author. And that was the primary focus of the relationship.

Q: I'm going to ask you again: Did you consider at the end of the trial that you were his friend?

A: I don't know how to answer that. I felt terrible when he was convicted. If I hadn't considered him in some degree a friend, I suppose I would have felt happy he was convicted. Instead I felt real bad.

Q: Did you consider him your friend?

A: That's the best I can do, Mr. Bostwick.

Q: Would you take a look at Exhibit 36A again. . . . It says, "Goddamn it Jeff, one of the worst things about all this is how suddenly and totally all of your friends—self included—have been deprived of the pleasure of your company." Why was it so easy for you to know that you were his friend when you were writing him that letter, and you can't decide today whether you were his friend at the end of the trial?

A: Well, that was eight years ago, and my recollections were a lot fresher.

Q: You've just forgotten that you used to be his friend, right?

McGinniss's agony went on:

Q: "Total strangers can recognize within five minutes that you did not receive a fair trial." You didn't really believe that he didn't receive a fair trial, did you?

A: Well, I'm sure that that was an oversimplification,

and indeed it misstates the total strangers. How could they recognize anything within five minutes?

Q: I don't know. Why did you tell him that?

A: I don't know. Because, you know, Mr. Bostwick, when I write a letter it's like making a phone call. You just—

Q: You talk about what's in your heart, right?

A: You talk about—it's not like writing for publication.

Q: You say what comes to mind—isn't that right? What you really feel?

A: You take less care with the way you phrase things.

Bostwick's own carefully shaped narrative hewed close to its theme of cold betrayal. He relentlessly hammered home the idea that McGinniss's deception of MacDonald had been a matter of simple opportunism, and that the letters had been written in utter cynicism—to get material out of MacDonald and to lull any suspicions he might have which could imperil McGinniss's project. To nail down his harsh thesis, Bostwick prefaced his reading of excerpts from the letters with a reading of excerpts from newspaper interviews that McGinniss had given during his publicity tour for *Fatal Vision*, in which, evidently thinking himself safe from the vengefulness of a man locked up for life, he spoke of MacDonald with frank loathing. ("He is a very sick human being," he told one reporter, and, in response to another reporter's question, fixed the time of his realization of MacDonald's guilt as having actually occurred during the trial.)

Kornstein, in his friendly examination of McGinniss, three weeks later, did what he could to repair the damage. On the fair assumption that deceiving a few journalists during a book tour was a lesser offense than deceiving MacDonald for four years, Kornstein had McGinniss testify that he had misinformed the reporters. "Statements by me that I was convinced of MacDonald's guilt before the jury came back were not accurate reflections of the way things really were," McGinniss said, at Kornstein's prodding, and went on, "I just gave some simplistic short-hand answers which, no question about it, in two or three instances created an impression which is not—it's the way I wished it had been, more than the way it was." Kornstein also asked McGinniss, "In those letters in 1979, did you genuinely feel every emotion that you expressed?"

A: Yes, sir, I felt every emotion I expressed. I'm not that good a writer to fake something like that.

Q: Was there anything in those letters that you intended to be false?

A: Nothing I intended to be false.

Q: Was there anything in those letters that you intended to deceive MacDonald with?

A: If we're talking about these first six or nine months, no, sir. They were honest expressions of feelings that I had at the time.

In his cross-examination, Bostwick went straight for the exposed throat:

Q: You said yesterday . . . looking at the letters of the first six to nine months after the trial, [that] you never intended to deceive him. . . . *After* the first six to nine months, did you intend to deceive him?

A: Well, there certainly came a time when I was willing to let him continue to believe whatever he wanted to believe, so he wouldn't try to prevent me from finishing my book, yes, sir.

Q: Is the answer yes?

A: The answer could be interpreted that way, I suppose.

Q: By someone reading the letters, for instance.

A: Well, I'm sure it would be by yourself, sir. I don't know—other people might interpret it differently.

Bostwick went on to read from a letter from McGinniss to MacDonald dated April 14, 1982, written soon after MacDonald had been reincarcerated following an eighteen-month spell of freedom. (In July 1980, the Fourth Circuit Court had ruled favorably on MacDonald's appeal that he had been denied a speedy trial, and he was released. Then, in March 1982, the Supreme Court overturned the lower court's decision, and MacDonald went back to jail.) Bostwick continued, "Mr. McGinniss, you told your wife you were glad he was back in jail. Two weeks later, in this letter, you're telling him that you hope you'll be able to call him at home. Why?"

A: As I've already testified, I believe because I was encouraging him to not discourage me from finishing the book that I had put so much of my life into at that point. My commitment was to the book and to this truth.

Q: And it was O.K. to tell him something that you really didn't believe in the service of this truth?

A: I would say that falls into Mr. Wambaugh's category of untruth.

McGinniss's reference to Wambaugh's "category of untruth" concerned what everyone later agreed was the pivotal moment of the trial. As the cornerstone of his defense of McGinniss, Kornstein had gathered together a roster of well-known writers—members of what he called "the literary community" and Bostwick less delicately, if perhaps more accurately, called "the writing industry"—to come and testify that McGinniss's deception of MacDonald was standard operating procedure. Kornstein's original list of "experts on the author-subject relationship," included William F. Buckley, Jr., Tom Wolfe, Jimmy Breslin, Victor Navasky, J. Anthony Lukas, and Wambaugh, but only Buckley and Wambaugh actually testified; after their appearance, the judge, evidently feeling that the defense had taken enough punishment from itself, called a halt, and decreed that no more writers would be heard from.

Buckley came first. Kornstein asked him, "Based on custom, practice, and usage within the literary community and your own experience, what is the scope of the author's discretion to encourage self-deception on the part of the subject?"

A: Well, there again, that's an artistic question. If Senator [Alan] Cranston, let's say, while I was writing a biography about him, began to make references that sounded to me as though he had another wife living in Florida, I would from time to time return to that subject to encourage him to give me more details, but I wouldn't alert him to the fact that I was suddenly discovering that he was a bigamist. . . .

Q: Again, based on custom, practice, and usage within the literary community and your own experience, would it be appropriate or inappropriate to perhaps feign agreement with the principles of the subject in order to encourage further conversation?

A: Well, I think it would be appropriate, given the priorities. The priorities are to encourage the person you're writing about to tell you everything, and if that takes going down to a bar and having a beer with him, you go down to the bar and have a beer with him. If it means that you have to listen to three hours of boring, trivial matter of really no concern, you go ahead and do that. It's part of the ordeal of a writer in seeking to get all the facts, on the basis of which he makes his definitive evaluations.

In his cross-examination, Bostwick got right down to his enjoyable business:

Q: You're not trying to tell the jury that you believe that an author can lie to the subject of a book that he's writing about, are you?

A: Well, it all depends on what you mean by the word "lie."

Q: A lie is a false statement of fact, Mr. Buckley. I'm sorry you're having such a difficulty—

A: Well, look, look, look—

Q: I can try to give you the definition of the word "lie."

A: Look, it's not that easy. I've read Sissela Bok's book on lying, and it's not that easy. For instance, if the Gestapo arrives and says, "Was Judge Rea here? Where did he go?," and I said, "Well, he went that way," am I lying? Thomas Aquinas would say I was lying, a lot of other people would say I wasn't lying, I was simply defending an innocent life.

Bostwick continued to nudge Buckley toward the minefield.

Q: I'm simply asking you whether it's the custom and practice in the literary field for authors to lie to the subject in order to get more information out of them.

A: It would really depend on the situation. If, for instance, you were writing a book on somebody who was a renowned philanderer and he said, "I mean, you do think my wife is impossible, don't you?," you might say, "Yeah, I think she's very hard to get along with," simply for the purpose of lubricating the discussion in order to learn more information. . . .

Q: So if you have to, you'd go down and have a beer with the guy to get more information, right?

A: Yeah, right.

Q: And if you have to [you'll] listen to three hours of boring talk from the person to try to get more out of them, right?

A: That's right.

Q: And if you have to, you'll tell him something you don't really believe in order to be able to get more information from him, isn't that right?

A: Yes. That is right, understood in context.

Kornstein put Wambaugh through the same paces as he had put Buckley, and Wambaugh, astonishingly—as if he were not the same person who had written MacDonald such a bluntly honest letter—testified that misleading subjects was a kind of sacred duty of writers.

Q: Is there a custom or practice in the literary world about whether or not an author should disclose his views to his subject?

A: I believe that one should never disclose one's views, because it may shut off further communication.

Q: Has that ever happened in your experience?

A: Yes. Frequently [subjects] would ask me questions that if I answered them truthfully would shut off further communication.

Q: And how did you answer them?

A: I would tell an untruth if I had to.

Q: Can you give us an example?

A: Yes. In writing *The Onion Field*, I can recall one of the murderers asking me if I believed him when he said he didn't shoot the policeman, and I at that time had interviewed scores of witnesses and had a mountain of information, and I did not believe him, but I said that I did, because I wanted him to continue talking. Because my ultimate responsibility was not to that person, my responsibility was to the book.

In his cross-examination, Bostwick asked Wambaugh, "Would you tell an untruth here today?" Wambaugh replied, "No, sir."

Q: Why would you tell an untruth then but not now?
A: I wasn't under oath, to begin with.
Q: That's the difference?
A: No, sir. My job was to get at the truth for the purpose of telling a coherent story, so I had to encourage that person to do it. May I describe the difference between untruth and lie?

The distinction Wambaugh proposed—"A lie is something that's told with ill will or in bad faith that is not true," while an untruth is "part of a device wherein one can get at the actual truth"—only handed Bostwick another weapon. In his closing address to the jury, he was able to say mockingly, "Wambaugh—he was interesting. I was intrigued by his definition of lie and untruth, and it was just something about the way he did it that makes me think you might be, too. I'm not sure. *I* would always try to say, whenever I got caught telling a lie, 'Well, I really didn't mean it. It really wasn't a bad lie.' " Turning his attention to Buckley, Bostwick observed, "Now, Buckley didn't know what a lie was, actually. We had an interesting conversation about St. Thomas Aquinas and Sissela

Bok, but he wasn't sure what it was. My mother would have taught him if she were here, I'll tell you."

The debacle of Buckley's and Wambaugh's testimony illustrates a truth that many of us learn as children: the invariable inefficacy of the "Don't blame me—everybody does it" defense. Society mediates between the extremes of, on the one hand, intolerably strict morality and, on the other, dangerously anarchic permissiveness through an unspoken agreement whereby we are given leave to bend the rules of the strictest morality, provided we do so quietly and discreetly. Hypocrisy is the grease that keeps society functioning in an agreeable way, by allowing for human fallibility and reconciling the seemingly irreconcilable human needs for order and pleasure. When Buckley and Wambaugh said bluntly that it's all right to deceive subjects, they breached the contract whereby you never come right out and admit you have stretched the rules for your own benefit. You do it and shut up about it, and hope you don't get caught, because if you are caught no one—or no one who has any sense—will come forward and say he has done the same thing himself. When Kornstein, in his closing statement, said, "Buckley and Wambaugh testified that the task is to get the story, and that you do what is necessary to get the story," he was simply inviting the crushing lecture on decency that Bostwick was all too pleased to read him in *his* final argument. "What you heard here this morning was truly outrageous," Bostwick said, and went on:

> What's outrageous is that the defendant here, supposedly the protector of the First Amendment freedoms—freedom of speech, freedom of expression—has put experts on the stand who said, in Mr. Kornstein's own words, that

they must do whatever is necessary to write the book. Those were the words that he used: "whatever is necessary."

Those words have been used by dictators, tyrants, demagogues throughout history to rationalize what they have done. . . . We've just gone through a series of Congressional investigations where that was also one of the excuses: We had to do what was necessary. It was all right to lie, because it was necessary.

The experts said it's all right to tell the man something you don't believe in, as long as you're getting more information from him, for the sake of the project. I listened throughout the two and a half hours, astounded that that would be set forth in a courtroom as being the kind of principle that writers or lawyers or juries should be guided by. We cannot do whatever is necessary. We have to do what is right.

ON NOVEMBER 23, 1987, three months after the end of the trial, an agreement to settle the suit was reached, whereby McGinniss, conceding no wrong, pledged to give MacDonald three hundred and twenty-five thousand dollars, to be paid by an anonymous party, presumably the insurance company of McGinniss's publisher. As it happened, I was in California on the day of the settlement, for my first meeting with Bostwick—actually, I was in his office in Santa Monica, reading court documents while waiting for him to return from the settlement negotiations. Since the day that McGinniss called from Williamstown to break off our talks, I had been in a state of odd uncertainty about how to proceed. Odd, because in the past reporting had been something I did instinctively and easily: it was like going to the store before dinner to gather the ingredients for what you were going to cook. But with this project nothing was instinctive or easy. The store, which hitherto had been a vast, glutted American supermarket, had shrunk to a bare little grocery in a Third World country. I couldn't get my hands on anything. McGinniss had broken off relations with me, Kornstein never answered my telephone calls, McGinniss's friends wouldn't speak with me, and even the court stenographer from whom I had ordered a transcript of the trial seemed to be part of what I began to think of as a conspiracy of fate; she was never in her office, and the transcript didn't come and didn't come. As I waited for it, back in New York, I would sometimes walk over to the building where Kornstein had his office (it happened to be two blocks from where I lived) and peer wistfully into the lobby. As I fretted, I also ruminated about what had happened between me and McGinniss. What had I done to cause the man to think of me as another persecutor, rather than simply as a colleague who had come to discuss issues of common interest raised by his lawsuit? I realized that I had been unimaginative. When one is feeling as beleaguered as McGinniss must have been feeling, anything short of utter, empathic agreement will seem hostile and unfeeling. When one is in pain, one wants sympathy and reassurance, not abstract argument. And when one has maintained—as McGinniss and Kornstein and Buckley and Wambaugh had maintained—that the whole future of journalism may depend on the writer's freedom to dissemble, because otherwise the subject will flee, then one is fairly obliged to flee from a writer who doesn't seem all that convinced of the rightness of one's position. For McGinniss to have continued our interviews in the face of my skepticism would have been to repudiate his own position. It was logically imperative that he break off our interviews and leave me as empty-handed as he believed he would have been left if he had told MacDonald his true thoughts.

Now, in Bostwick's office, I felt the familiar stir of something I hadn't felt since my dismissal by McGinniss—something I recognized with delight, like the return of appetite after an illness. This was the feeling of gratified vanity that American journalism all but guarantees its practitioners when they are out reporting. In our society, the journalist ranks with the philanthropist as a person who has something extremely valuable to dispense (his currency is the strangely intoxicating substance called publicity), and who is consequently treated with a deference quite out of proportion to his merits as a person. There are very few people in this country who do not regard with rapture the prospect of being written about or being interviewed on a radio or television program. Even someone as smart and self-possessed as Bostwick said yes to me when I telephoned him from New York to ask if I could interview him and his client. His first step in the minuet was to say that his side of the lawsuit had not been fairly represented in the press, and that he hoped I would be more fair-minded. My first step, since I did not want to lose him and MacDonald as I had lost Kornstein and McGinniss, was to say that fairness was an ideal rather than something one could give or withhold at will—and anyway it was not a quality that writers had a very big stake in cultivating. He then murmured his appreciation of this "honest" answer—with which, of course, I had simply taken ingratiation to a higher level. Throughout my stay in California, I maintained the posture of the bluntly honest reporter who says what she thinks and never tells a Wambaughian untruth. I believe that the meaning (or meaninglessness) of this posture was completely understood by Bostwick and his associates, and, later, by MacDonald and his various friends and followers. I think that by the time I arrived on the scene everyone involved in the MacDonald-McGinniss lawsuit had become thoroughly familiar with the deepest structures of the journalist-subject encounter, and was under no illusions about a new journalist with a new cover story. But how many of us with no illusions left about the nature of romantic love will for that reason turn down a plausible lover when one comes along? Don't a rare few affairs *not* turn out badly? And isn't the latest lover invariably different in kind from all the previous ones?

In Bostwick's office, I knew it wasn't only the fine California climate that was giving me such a feeling of well-being. The metaphor of the love affair applies to both sides of the journalist-subject equation, and the journalist is no less susceptible than the subject to its pleasures and excitements. In our talk and in the transcript of the trial, McGinniss had made a point of distinguishing between the reporting and the writing phases of the journalistic enterprise, speaking of them almost as if the one had nothing to do with the other, and as if the reporting and the writing were done by two different people. While this confession of doubleness was McGinniss's undoing at the trial—the contradiction between the nice guy who had lived in the fraternity house with MacDonald and had written to him in prison and the coldhearted "best-selling author" of *Fatal Vision* was simply too grotesque—it is in fact an accurate description of the general journalistic case. An abyss lies between the journalist's experience of being out in the world talking to people and his experience of being alone in a room writing. When the interviews are over and the journalist first faces the labor of writing, he feels no less resentful than the subject will feel when he reads the finished text. Sometimes the labor seems particularly hard. In 1985, in answer to an interrogatory by the plaintiff, McGinniss wrote of "too many sleepless nights, too many terrible dreams, too many blank, dull, empty mornings spent staring out the back window of my house, cold coffee in hand, postponing for another minute, another five, another ten, the dreadful task of going back upstairs and again confronting the chilling realization which, against my will, was forming itself. . . ." The realization was that MacDonald had murdered his wife and children; but no writer can read this passage without recognizing in it the feeling of not wanting to get to work on something that may not come out well—and McGinniss had special reason to feel anxious about how *Fatal Vision* would come out.

But now, as I waited for Bostwick, the problem of writing was for me, as it had been for McGinniss in the early days of his encounter with MacDonald, like the problem of death: it did not interfere with the pleasures of the present. From Bostwick's repeated references to his mother in the trial transcript and from the sound of his friendly, Plains States voice on the telephone, I had formed an image of him as a distinctly salt-of-the-earth type, and had imagined his office as being fittingly unpretentious: a couple of amiably seedy rooms, say, over a diving-equipment-rental shop on a commercial drag. The actual Bostwick office, in a building at the westernmost end of Wilshire Boulevard, was a place of the most advanced and sleekly expensive design. Beyond a reception room where Mozart was playing on a tape deck and an elegantly dressed receptionist sat at a light-gray counter, a conference room furnished with a lacquer table and ten chairs of a vaguely Oriental design was visible through a glass wall, and beyond that was a breathtaking view of the Pacific, which looked as if it, too, had come from an authoritative postmodern design firm.

Bostwick had put a room at my disposal, where I could peruse a looseleaf book of trial exhibits, which were not yet in the public domain, and had assigned an assistant to look after me. Toward noon, he called in to say that the case was settled. That evening, Bostwick, his wife, Janette (a pretty, delicately boned, soft-spoken woman, who is a Gestalt therapist), and I went out to dinner together at a restaurant near the office. The occasion had a light, celebratory atmosphere. Bostwick reminisced about the early days of the case. "When MacDonald first came to us, we told him that his libel case was worthless because he was libel-proof," he said. "How can you damage the reputation of someone who has been convicted of murder? But when MacDonald gave us his letters from McGinniss, immediately on reading them—since we already had the news articles in which McGinniss told reporters he had decided MacDonald was guilty during the trial—we said, 'This is a classic case of fraud.' I took a deposition from McGinniss in 1985, and after an hour in the room with him I knew we had him. I just rubbed my hands with glee from that day forward, because I knew what I could do on cross-examination. It wouldn't even have to be a very good cross-examination.

"That first deposition was in New York," Bostwick went on, "and then, a year later, I followed it up with another, in Pittsfield, Massachusetts, which is close to Williamstown. McGinniss had refused to come to New

York for the second part of his deposition. He said, 'Last time, I was courteous to you and came to New York. This time, you're going to have to do it in Massachusetts.' The law says that you can't drag a person too far from his home, so I went. As it turned out, it was a great trip. It was late October, just after the Mets had won the World Series. My flight went right up the Hudson to Albany, and it was the most beautiful plane ride I've ever had. It was a crystal-clear day. From Albany I drove to Pittsfield. Kornstein had a much harder time getting there. He left Manhattan about the same time I left Los Angeles. It was more trouble for him that it was for me." Bostwick laughed. "Can you imagine lawyers posturing over this sort of thing—'Well, they won a victory on that one, making us go to Massachusetts'? That happens so much in this business you'd be shocked. People fight bitterly over these things, and then find themselves waist-deep in mud and asking themselves, 'How did I get here? What happened?' You acted like an ass, that's what happened. Sometimes I wonder about being a lawyer. I wasn't always one—I was a Peace Corps volunteer and a translator and an engineer and an Army officer first."

Bostwick traded his empty plate for his wife's half-full one, and as he took an appreciative forkful of blackened catfish he said, "McGinniss said he owed it to Colette and to the kids to write the book, but—as I said in my closing argument—it wasn't them he owed, it was the Bank of New England. If you read those letters to MacDonald, you'll see that he was in financial trouble the whole time. That's why he had to keep deceiving MacDonald into cooperating with him until he could write his best-seller. He had taken the publisher's advance and spent it. He wasn't free to tell MacDonald the truth."

I was interested to see that, even though the lawsuit was settled, Bostwick was still in the grip of the dislike and contempt for the defendant which had informed his work in the courtroom. Evidently, to be a good trial lawyer you have to be a good hater. A lawsuit is to ordinary life what war is to peacetime. In a lawsuit, everybody on the other side is bad. A trial transcript is a discourse in malevolence.

I asked if Bostwick didn't think it possible that McGinniss *had* been telling the truth in his letters to MacDonald—that he had loved him as well as hated him.

Bostwick, as if suddenly remembering that he was no longer in the courtroom and could relent toward his adversary without risk to his side, nodded agreement. "Things weren't simple for him. He had conflicted emotions."

Janette, who hadn't spoken very much, now said, "In my work, a patient will come in and say, 'This is the truth about me.' Then, later in the therapy, a significant and entirely opposite truth may emerge—but they're both true."

"It's the same with the judicial process," Bostwick said. "People feel that it's a search for truth. But I don't think that is its function in this society. I'm convinced that its function is cathartic. It's a means for allowing people to air their differences, to let them feel as if they had a forum. You release tension in the social body in some way, whether or not you come to the truth."

"But in a criminal trial," I said, introducing the subject to which every discussion of the MacDonald-McGinniss lawsuit inevitably leads, "isn't there only one truth? Didn't MacDonald either commit these murders or not commit them?"

"I don't believe he did," Bostwick said, "and I wouldn't have taken the case if I thought he had. I probably explained it best to my daughter when she started being harassed at school because of my involvement in the case. I said to her, 'Look, nobody knows. I'm not saying I *know* he didn't do it. Only God and Dr. MacDonald know, and neither of them is talking. But I *believe* he didn't do it. His descriptions of the four intruders matched people seen within five or six miles of his house a couple of hours before the murders. I've never had it explained to me how he was able to describe those people."

At the trial, Bostwick had pressed McGinniss on his certainty that MacDonald had committed the murders, reading aloud a passage from *Fatal Vision* in which McGinniss, referring to MacDonald's mother, wrote, "There were too many things I could not say [to her], for instance that I knew her son had killed his wife and children." Then Bostwick said to McGinniss, "You don't really *know* he killed his wife and children, do you?" The exchange continued:

A: Well, I know that he's been convicted, and the conviction has been confirmed by every appeals court that's considered it.

Q: That's not what it says in here, though, Mr. McGinniss. That's why I asked you the question in your own words. You don't really *know*, do you?

A: I know to my own satisfaction, yes, after the four years of intensive investigation I did.

Q: Did you ever talk to anyone who you believe *knows* that Dr. MacDonald committed the crimes?

A: Well, the victims are dead. Can't talk to them. And I came to believe that MacDonald simply didn't tell the truth.

Q: Have you ever talked to anyone who *knows* that Dr. MacDonald committed the crimes?

A: Well, I think you're getting into an area of epistemology here, Mr. Bostwick.

Q: That's right. I agree with you.

A: Yes.

Q: Did you ever talk to anyone who knows?

A: I couldn't talk to Colette. Couldn't talk to Kimberly.

Q: Did you talk to anyone who *knows*, Mr. McGinniss?

A: Yes, I did.

Q: Who did you talk to?

A: I talked to MacDonald.

Q: You know that he knows?

A: I know in my heart that he knows.

Q: Did he ever tell you that he did?

A: He certainly didn't.

Now, at the restaurant, Bostwick spoke of his own willingness to live with doubt. "Given the facts as I know them—and there's a lot of evidence on both sides—I prefer being uncertain to taking the easy way out and getting rid of my discomfort by being absolutely certain. I don't *know*, and no one on this earth can be absolutely certain of the truth here. Anyone who professes to be absolutely certain I really distrust."

MY FIRST sight of MacDonald—which took place the next day—was of a tall, well-built man in a light-blue cotton jumpsuit negotiating a feat of poise. A prisoner at Terminal Island is brought to the visitors' room in handcuffs; he is released from them when he puts his wrists through a slot in a barred door so a guard on the other side can remove them. Meeting a visitor under these circumstances would not seem to offer much scope for a soigné entrance, but MacDonald somehow managed to get through the humiliating ritual as if he were an actor swiftly shedding his costume before greeting friends in the green room, rather than a prisoner coming out of solitary confinement for a few hours. He had been transferred to Terminal Island from the federal prison in Arizona where he was serving out his sentence so that he could attend the McGinniss trial, and had not yet been sent back. During the trial, for bureaucratic reasons, he had been kept "in the hole" at the prison, and was still being held there. His cell was five feet by nine, and was furnished with a bunk bed and a toilet; he was allowed out for exercise for one hour a day.

MacDonald and I sat facing each other across a small, plastic-topped table in a very small room that was separated from an identical visitors' room (which remained unoccupied) by a glass partition. The rules had changed at Terminal Island, and journalists were now allowed to bring in notebooks and tape recorders; thus a tape recorder sat on the table between us. MacDonald had brought a clipboard to which a thick sheaf of papers was attached, and he talked rapidly and relentlessly, like an executive or a politician with a prepared line of patter always at the ready; he used "we" a lot, instead of "I." However, unlike many compulsive talkers, who regard what you may occasionally say as an annoying interruption, he would fall silent and pay very close attention whenever I spoke. I could almost feel the intensity of his listening, and I was struck by his intelligence as an interlocutor. Only gradually would the string of his interest in what I was saying slacken and would he relapse into the old, armored, obsessed, aggressive story—"unjust conviction," "biased judge," "suppressed evidence," "new witnesses"—by which his existence had been shaped for the eight years since his conviction.

Both in the prepared story and in his unpremeditated responses MacDonald used language that was at curious odds with his person: he himself bristled with tense aliveness, but his language was dead, flat, soft, clichéd, unnuanced. The discrepancy became even more marked when, back in my hotel room, I listened to the tape recordings I had made in the prison. Isolated and stripped of the man's strong gestural presence, the plain words had an awful puerility. In *Fatal Vision*, a great many pages are given over to excerpts from the tape recordings that MacDonald made for McGinniss in prison, and I recognized the language: "The year at Princeton was incredibly great," a section entitled "The Voice of Jeffrey MacDonald" begins, and goes on, "I was in absolute love with Colette and I thought having Kimberly was neat and we had tons of people over to the house."

A few months after seeing MacDonald, I had dinner with Michael Malley, and at the end of the evening he brought up the problem of MacDonald's speech. "Language is not one of Jeff's skills," he said. "He doesn't express his feelings well, and he doesn't express subtleties. If I were to remake Jeffrey MacDonald, I'd start with his language—simply to make him more expressive. Language is what makes people human, and it is the primary way we have of knowing who other people are. I think there were two reasons why Jeff lost the criminal trial. One was that the judge hamstrung us in the evidence we could present. And the other reason was Jeff. He didn't have the ability to make the jury believe him. This is an idea that Jeff doesn't like. He thinks he tells his story well. But I always say to him, 'The best time I ever heard you tell your story was at the Army hearing, when you broke down and stopped talking, when you couldn't go on talking'—and that grizzled Army colonel and those three Army officers sitting up there with him choked back their sobs."

At the time of the dinner—in April 1988—I was in correspondence with MacDonald, and in my next letter I took the occasion of the meeting with Malley to delicately broach the subject of his speech and ask if he himself had any sense of it as a problem. MacDonald's reply ran to fourteen pages. He wrote, in part:

> Your comments re: me being vivid in person but not so in letters and transcripts surprises me only a little. . . . If I come across as guarded, surely the major factor must be the fact that I'm wrongly accused and convicted. And every sentence I've said in my defense, or *didn't* say in my defense, has been exhaustively analyzed. My gestures, my words, my letters, my dreams, my memory—*all* have been dissected publicly and privately, and I began to feel *nothing* but tiny portions of my memory are sacred anymore. . . .
>
> I personally feel the hair on the back of my neck rise when you ask this question, because (to me) inherent in the question is a defense of Joe McGinniss's outrageous intentional mis-portrayal. What the question seems to say is "Jeff is partially responsible for Joe's admittedly not-too-accurate portrayal." I think that is pure bunk, a total cop-out for his complete & utter failure to be truthful and accurate. . . . McGinniss should have to answer for his lies, his deceit, his fraudulent actions, his misreporting. . . . Surely writers rarely, if ever, have had *greater* access to a subject, excepting husband/wife teams. Not only did we meet, dine, talk, correspond, interact over four years—but we lived together, he had access to an entire lifetime of correspondence, and he had total access to every

single friend & acquaintance of any importance at all in my life. In addition, he acted as part of my *defense* team, for God's sake, a situation where every conceivable vulnerability is dissected over & over ad nauseam. In addition, he saw me under extreme stress, and had total access to many others who lived or worked with me under other conditions of stress.

So McGinnis has *no* excuse for his false portrayal. He wasn't watching a distant subject through a haze—he was deeply involved, as "best friend," for four years—and still managed to miss the entire core of my being.

I did not press MacDonald further on the subject of his speech. Later, on rereading the transcript of the McGinniss trial, I came across a section of testimony that, had I remembered it, would have made me think twice before suggesting to MacDonald that there was something funny about his speech. This was the testimony of the psychiatrist Michael Stone, who had been hired by Kornstein to confirm the truth of McGinniss's theory, expressed in *Fatal Vision*, that MacDonald suffered from the Kernbergian complaint of pathological narcissism. (In his cross-examination, Bostwick was able to point out that pathological narcissism does not appear in the *Diagnostic and Statistical Manual of Mental Disorders* of the American Psychiatric Association—which, however, doesn't mean that the disorders that do appear are any less questionable; our standard psychiatric diagnostic nomenclature has all the explanatory power of the nomenclature of medieval physiology involving the four humors.) Although Stone, a graduate of the Columbia Psychoanalytic Institute and a professor of clinical psychiatry at Cornell University Medical College, had never examined (or even met) MacDonald, he was in no doubt, after reading the six-hundred-

nscript of the tape recordings MacDonald had
or McGinniss, that the man suffered from some-
even worse than pathological narcissism—namely,
"malignant narcissism, which is . . . like pathological
narcissism-plus." Stone told the jury that he had made a
concordance of the "various abnormal traits and qualities
and examples" he had found in the transcript, but that
"the most impressive bit of evidence vis-à-vis pathological
narcissism . . . is not what is on any given page but what
is *not* in any of the pages."

"What do you mean by that?" Kornstein inquired.

Stone replied, "In all of this, there is nothing that
touches one as genuine about either [MacDonald] or anybody else, with the possible exception of his own peevish-
ness and propensity to anger when his will is thwarted.
But, apart from that, no one comes alive for the reader. I
read this material twice. I have, as I say, made a concordance tool. I couldn't tell you what Colette was really like;
I couldn't tell you what Kimmy was really like. . . . None
of them come alive; they're all stiff figures. And that is an
amazing thing to experience when reading six hundred
pages of autobiographical material."

In writing to MacDonald that "less comes through about
you in your writing and in transcripts of your speech than
is usual," I had made the same error that Stone made in
marvelling at MacDonald's incapacity for rendering Tol-
stoyan portraits of himself and his family. MacDonald's
bland dullness on tape seemed unusual to me and to Stone
(and also to McGinniss, who had told me how he groaned
whenever a new tape arrived from the prison) because of
its contrast to the excitingly dire character of the crime
for which he stood convicted: a murderer shouldn't sound
like an accountant. But in fact—as every journalist will

confirm—MacDonald's uninterestingness is not unusual at all. In Philip Roth's experimental novel *The Counterlife*, the novelist-narrator Zuckerman observes:

> People don't turn themselves over to writers as full-blown literary characters—generally they give you very little to go on and, after the impact of the initial impression, are barely any help at all. Most people (beginning with the novelist—himself, his family, just about everyone he knows) are absolutely unoriginal, and his job is to make them appear otherwise. It's not easy. If Henry was ever going to turn out to be interesting, I was going to have to do it.

However, when a journalist fetches up against someone like Henry ("naïve and uninteresting" and "perfectly ordinary" is Zuckerman's description of him), all he can do—since his job is to report, not to invent—is flee from him and hope that a more suitable subject will turn up soon. For while the novelist, when casting about for a hero or a heroine, has all of human nature to choose from, the journalist must limit his protagonists to a small group of people of a certain rare, exhibitionistic, self-fabulizing nature, who have already done the work on themselves that the novelist does on his imaginary characters—who, in short, present themselves as ready-made literary figures. In the MacDonald-McGinniss case we have an instance of a journalist who apparently found out too late (or let himself find out too late) that the subject of his book was not up to scratch—not suitable for a work of nonfiction, not a member of the wonderful race of auto-fictionalizers, like Joseph Mitchell's Joe Gould and Truman Capote's Perry Smith, on whom the New Journalism and the "nonfiction novel" depend for their life. MacDonald was simply a guy like the rest of us, with nothing to offer but a tedious and improbable story about his innocence of a bad crime. In the normal course of things, McGinniss would probably have quickly recognized MacDonald's ordinariness, abandoned the project of writing about him, and once again taken up the search for the larger-than-life subject that is as crucial to a journalist's work as the quest for a rare image is crucial to the photographer's art. But, for various reasons, McGinniss chose not to see what was staring him in the face. One reason, it may be assumed, was his old weakness for being "inside"; the offer of being privy to conversations that no other outsider could hear, of having "access" to MacDonald that would be withheld from others, was no doubt irresistible to him. Another was the pressure of MacDonald's desire to be written about. As my reading of the transcript of MacDonald's prison tapes has shown me what poor McGinniss was up against in trying to fashion a Raskolnikov out of a Jeffrey MacDonald, so have my relations with MacDonald himself permitted me to feel some of the man's seductiveness and to understand why McGinniss would have succumbed to its force. By the time McGinniss was fully aware that MacDonald would not work out as a character—and one of the leitmotivs of McGinniss's letters to MacDonald in prison is his constant attempt to prod him into being interesting, even to the point of trying to stir him up by revealing a number of sexual indiscretions of his own (which Bostwick took great pleasure in reading out loud in the courtroom)—he was too deeply implicated in the process whereby a piece of writing is transformed into a commodity, and also too heavily in personal debt. (His money problems—his need for a mortgage and a new furnace and so on—are another leitmotiv of the correspondence.)

The solution McGinniss arrived at for dealing with MacDonald's characterlessness was not a satisfactory one, but it had to do. At the criminal trial, the prosecution had argued that it did not have to show that MacDonald was the kind of person who could have committed the crimes— it had only to show that he had indeed committed them— but this was precisely what McGinniss, the nonfiction novelist, *did* have to show. The means he adopted was to quote long descriptions by Kernberg and Lasch of their vivid characters, the pathological narcissists, his idea evidently being that some of the aura of those characters would come off on MacDonald—that, by extension, their interesting horribleness would become his. When Kernberg (in a passage quoted by McGinniss) speaks of pathological narcissists' "grandiosity, extreme self-centeredness, and remarkable absence of interest and empathy for others, in spite of the fact that they are so very eager to obtain admiration and approval," and adds,

> They feel that they have the right to control and possess others and to exploit them without guilt feelings, and, behind a surface which very often is charming and engaging, one senses coldness and ruthlessness,

he could be talking about the sinister Grandcourt in *Daniel Deronda* and Osmond in *Portrait of a Lady*. Unfortunately for McGinniss's project, however, there is nothing in the preceding six hundred pages of *Fatal Vision* to suggest that Kernberg was talking about Jeffrey MacDonald; nor does McGinniss's quotation from Lasch on the narcissist's "boundless rage against the female sex," based on his "fear of the devouring mother of the pre-Oedipal fantasy," connect with anything McGinniss could show MacDonald to have done.

Hervey Cleckley's psychopath worked a little better for McGinniss. *The Mask of Sanity*, first published in 1941, is an extremely odd book, which begins (to give an idea of its period flavor) with an attack on *Finnegans Wake* and includes among its vignettes of anti-social behavior the case of an "intelligent and in some respects distinguished young man" who was discovered having sex with four black "unwashed laborers" in a tourist cabin in the South. For some reason, this quaint and rather mad book continues to exert its hold on the imaginations of American psychiatrists; it appeared in a fifth edition as recently as 1976, and is still used as a textbook in medical schools throughout the country. The book's thesis, which is buried among masses of the sort of thing cited above, is that there is a kind of evildoer called a psychopath, who does not seem in any way abnormal or different from other people but in fact suffers from "a grave psychiatric disorder," whose chief symptom is the very appearance of normality by which the horror of his condition is obscured. For behind "the mask of sanity" there is not a real human being but a mere simulacrum of one. Cleckley writes:

> We are dealing here not with a complete man at all but with something that suggests a subtly constructed reflex machine which can mimic the human personality perfectly. This smoothly operating psychic apparatus not only reproduces consistently specimens of good human reasoning but also appropriate simulations of normal human emotion in

response to nearly all the varied stimuli of life. So perfect is this reproduction of a whole and normal man that no one who examines him can point out in scientific or objective terms why he is not real. And yet one knows or feels he knows that reality, in the sense of full, healthy experiencing of life, is not here.

Cleckley's "grave psychiatric disorder" is, of course, the same disorder that afflicted Count Dracula, Frankenstein's monster, and a host of other wonderful literary creations. The attempt to solve the problem of evil and perpetuate the Romantic myth of the innate goodness of man through the fanciful notion that the people who commit evil acts are lacking in the usual human equipment—are not "real" human beings at all but soulless monsters—is a familiar topos of Victorian Romantic literature. That Cleckley's book remains to this day a serious psychiatric text is a testament to the strength of this fantasy among psychiatrists. To McGinniss, the concept of the psychopath did not so much offer a solution to his literary problem of making MacDonald a believable murderer as give him permission to evade the problem—just as the concept itself evades the problem it purports to solve. To say that people who do bad things don't seem bad is to say something we all already know: no one flaunts bad behavior, everyone tries to hide it, every villain wears a mask of goodness. The concept of the psychopath is, in fact, an admission of failure to solve the mystery of evil—it is merely a restatement of the mystery—and only offers an escape valve for the frustration felt by psychiatrists, social workers, and police officers, who daily encounter its force. For McGinniss, the Cleckley tautology must also have offered a way out of his moral dilemma in regard to MacDonald. If Mac-

Donald only seemed to be a fellow human being, and was actually a "subtly constructed reflex machine" (wearing a mask? Cleckley never quite got the bugs out of his figural machinery), then McGinniss owed him nothing, and could betray him with impunity, since he was betraying not "him" but only some sort of unholy "it."

When I returned to New York from California, I telephoned Dr. Stone. At the trial, he had attempted to fuse Cleckley's Dracula with Kernberg's Grandcourt in his diagnostic portrait of MacDonald, achieving rather odd results. Now, on the phone, he said he welcomed the opportunity to enlarge on his testimony—he had a *great deal* to tell me, he said—and a few days later I opened the door to his office, on the ground floor of an apartment building on Central Park West. The office was like a Victorian parlor—or perhaps like a stage set for one—furnished with a grand piano, velvet draperies, Persian rugs, brocaded sofas and chairs, ornate inlaid tables, books in old leather bindings, and dimly glowing lamps. Stone, a tall, loosely built man in his middle fifties, with a kindly, soft, rosy face and white hair, motioned for me to sit on one of the brocaded sofas in front of a low marble-topped table, and seated himself nearby in a bentwood rocker.

Stone's eagerness to talk to me had been preceded by his eagerness to testify for the defense. At the trial, under Bostwick's cross-examination, he had had to concede that in his first telephone conversation with Kornstein—before he had seen any of the transcripts on which he based his testimony—he had all but agreed to testify. In reply to a question about his fee as an expert witness, he told Bostwick he had not yet determined the fee, because "I have spent upwards of nineteen hundred hours, and I feel that some of that has been out of a special interest on my part," and that "no one asked me to make a concordance of six hundred pages of material. I did that myself to help orient things in my own mind, and I feel that I will charge a lower amount as a result." Now, in his office, Stone said, "I had read *Fatal Vision* years before, and it was pretty clear that Jeff MacDonald was a very pathological person."

"You thought that from reading the book?" I asked.

"Oh, sure. The man was at the very least a pathological liar, and since he was also a killer, that made him a very ugly and obnoxious person—a threat to the body social, and clearly a very sick personality. However, I had not paid too much attention to this when I read the book—it was just another interesting book. By the time they asked me to look into the matter as a personality-disorder expert, I had become a—if you will—murderologist, as a hobby. I had amassed a large collection of psychobiographies of murderers, and I was much more familiar with the famous killers of the past twenty or thirty years than I had been when I read the book. The whole subject had become very intriguing to me, so I was very enthusiastic about participating in the trial. They sent me a transcription of the thirty tapes of Jeff MacDonald talking while in jail—his pseudo-autobiography. It was all fake."

"Fake?"

"Well, the whole thing was a tissue of hyperbole and outright lies and deceit. I made an index of the examples of lying, self-aggrandizement, boasting, et cetera, page by page, so I would be better prepared at the trial to cite chapter and verse for anything they might ask me. It is a remarkable exercise in lying. Now, knowing full well that I couldn't admit this into evidence—the law is adversarial in structure, and thus antithetical to scientific method—I nevertheless conducted a little experiment, just to see if I was on the right track. After reading the hundreds and hundreds of pages of the transcript, I took four pages at random and had my secretary Xerox a dozen copies, which I gave to the class at Cornell that I teach on personality disorders. The students are Ph.D. psychologists and young psychiatrists. I didn't tell them anything except 'Here are four pages from a tape recording that somebody made about his life. Here is a list of the *DSM-III* standard diagnostic personality disorders. Please scribble down whether you think the person's words convey any evidence pertaining to the presence of one or several of these disorders.' And everyone picked up that he was narcissistic, and most that he was anti-social—just from the four pages! And my wife picked it up from *one* page, because I had the stuff lying on the bed one evening, and she glanced at it and said, 'My God, who is this narcissistic son of a bitch?' Ha, ha! Just like that! Of course, at the trial they asked me, 'How can you diagnose a person you haven't examined?' Often, you can't, but with personality disorders you can sometimes do a better job when you haven't examined the person than when you have, because the subject is going to lie through his teeth. Kernberg's concept of pathological narcissism is nothing more than the confluence of narcissistic traits—poor empathy, self-aggrandizement, manipulative and exploitive use of others—with anti-social qualities like ruthlessness, conning people, hurting others, taking liberties with the rules by which society regulates itself. So it was not surprising that my wife and my dozen students could make the diagnosis at the snap of a finger. However, I couldn't introduce my experiment into evidence, because it was hearsay. It bothered the hell out of me. Here was a man who by the best scientific standards was exactly what Joe McGinniss said he was, and yet I couldn't introduce that evidence into court."

I said that it seemed to me his experiment was hardly up to the best—or any—scientific standards, since it had no controls.

"Yes," Stone said, "I could have gone about it in that scrambled way, using several normal people—somebody with a different personality disorder, some other convicted person—along with Jeff MacDonald. But none of that could have been admitted into evidence unless the other side had overseen the experiment, and they would never have agreed to do that because they know bloody well that inside he's exactly the way the book says he is."

"This is your belief, but you haven't established it."

"No. But I suspect strongly that Bostwick knew he wasn't dealing with Lord Fauntleroy."

"You don't feel that there is any possibility that Mac-Donald is innocent?"

"No. In fact—and this, too, was something I wasn't able to say in court, since Bostwick cleverly ate up all the time with a bunch of silly questions and I had to catch a plane—the four intruders who MacDonald claimed were responsible for the murders represented the only truth, psychologically speaking, that he told. There really *were* four people who intruded on the hedonistic life style and whoring around of Jeff MacDonald: the four people who intruded on his disinclination to be a responsible husband and father; namely, Colette, Kristen, Kimberly, and the unborn son. Three white and one black—the hidden one."

Stone went on to speak of having seen MacDonald in the courtroom. "I was highly nervous about being in the presence of this man," he said. "I had the feeling his eyes could bore holes through a tank. The steely stare of this hostile man! I made a point of finding out when he would be paroled, and when I learned that it was after the time I would be no longer be on earth I felt bolder."

"You talk about him as if you really knew him, as if he were a real person," I said. "But actually he's a character in a book. Everything we know about him we know from McGinniss's text."

Stone said nothing for a moment, and I wondered whether my remark had been imprudent. In asking a character in one text to comment on the ontological status of a character in another text, was I alerting Stone too soon—as I had alerted McGinniss too soon—to the dangers of subjecthood? Stone wavered, but—obviously made of hardier metal than McGinniss—resolutely went on with his mission of self-disclosure. "He's not a Dickens character," he finally said, correctly, if irrelevantly.

"You really don't like him," I said.

"No. It's hard to like a man who stabs his pregnant wife to death. It takes more—what shall I say?—love of mankind than I possess. I'm more of the school of 'You get what you earn, and you have to earn what you get.' "

Stone had spoken earlier of the chain of abuse and brutalization that links generations of violent people. I asked him, "Isn't it possible that bad things were done to MacDonald in his early years? That his childhood wasn't all that idyllic, and that he repressed what happened?"

"Yes."

"If you knew that to be so, would you feel more benign toward him?"

"No."

"Why not?"

"Because he's a liar. Because he's not man enough to

say, 'I committed those murders because I was under the influence of amphetamines. I didn't know what I was doing. Colette was taking a course in psychology, she was going to wear the pants in the family. This was threatening to me; I felt left out. I was beginning to fondle the older girl too much, and she caught me'—this is Colette's stepfather's theory; he told me about it during the trial—'so in a moment of frenzied feeling that ruined my whole life I just killed the whole lot of them.' If he could say all that, I'd still want him put away for the rest of his life, but at least I'd have some respect for the fact that he could be honest about what happened. No way. He can't do that. He's not built to do that."

"You take a very harsh view, which is unusual for a psychotherapist in our culture."

"Unfortunately, it *is* unusual. I am at odds with many of my colleagues as a result of that. I feel that the profession has too much of this '*Tout comprendre, tout pardonner*' attitude. And there is also the 'We can fix it' attitude—the notion that if we can send a man to the moon surely we can make a psychopath go straight. But a person who has a propensity to murder is beyond the pale of psychotherapy. It is folly to think that a person like that could be corrected through the process of one-to-one therapy. He is a lost soul."

As MICHAEL STONE's office had astonished and mystified me, so did Ray Shedlick's windowless office in a security firm on the outskirts of Durham, North Carolina, seem immediately familiar, with its dark-wood panelling, framed certificates, athletic trophies, and a poignant sort of bareness and neatness—the emblems of rural American officialdom. Shedlick, a retired New York City police detective, was hired by MacDonald in 1982 as an investigator. A tall, slender man of fifty-five, with a very agreeable manner, wearing a red jersey shirt and tinted glasses, he had met me at the Durham airport on a Saturday in the winter of 1988 and driven me to the empty office building, a few miles away, where we now sat waiting for a third member of the party, a writer and professor named Jeffrey Elliot, who taught at nearby North Carolina Central University. Elliot was preparing a book on the MacDonald case and had appeared in the McGinniss trial as a rebuttal witness to Buckley and Wambaugh. Bostwick was at first reluctant to call him—a man who was writing a book on MacDonald did not seem to be the wisest choice as an expert on the author-subject relationship. But MacDonald was very insistent that he do so, and after speaking with Elliot on the telephone Bostwick changed his mind, realizing that he had stumbled upon a treasure. He would not have been able to invent a witness who would better embody the high-mindedness he sought to hold up as an alternative to the ruthless expediency that Buckley and Wambaugh declared to be the standard in the writing profession.

"Dr. Elliot," Bostwick said in his examination (Elliot has a doctorate in political science), "do you have an opinion as to whether an author who is attempting to obtain information from a living subject he is going to write about may tell that living subject something that in fact the author does not believe to be true, in order to obtain more information from the subject?" (The clumsiness of Bostwick's syntax derived from a series of objections by Kornstein to earlier versions of the question, in which the word "lie" was used; they were sustained, forcing Bostwick into these contortions.)

Elliot replied, "My opinion is that, while I'm sure there are those who do this, it is extremely irregular and unprofessional and, in my view, lacking in integrity and principle. I have not done it. I would not do it. And most authors whom I have interviewed, whom I know, whom I work with, would not deceive or lie or tell false-hoods, either in terms of getting assignments or, once they receive the assignments, of manipulating their sub-jects in order to write a story that they thought would fetch them either greater money or greater notoriety. Such conduct would likely result, particularly if discov-ered, in a ruination of reputations, publishers, and pub-lishing houses, and would destroy credibility in terms of getting future assignments and projects." He continued, "Obviously, if one expects to interview well-known in-ternational and national figures, an attitude of hostility or belligerency is certainly going to kill the interview be-fore it begins. But that's very, very different from ex-pressing directly—either verbally or in writing—untruths which lead the subject to believe that in fact you have one position when you have another. That, I think, is just unacceptable."

In his cross-examination, Kornstein, attempting to show that Elliot, when it came to the point, was no better than Wambaugh or Buckley, brought up an interview with Fi-del Castro that Elliot had done for *Playboy* in 1985, and asked, "Now, when you were interviewing Fidel Castro, you didn't tell him that you were against his Cuban rev-olution, did you?"

"No, I did not," Elliot replied.

"And you didn't tell him that you thought he was a mass murderer, did you?"

"I did not."

"In fact, didn't you try to appear sensitive and understanding of his particular point of view?"

"Sensitive and understanding and willing to listen."

"Right. You were not confrontational?" Kornstein said, forgetting the first rule of cross-examination: Ask only questions you know the answers to.

"Yes, I was," Elliot replied. "There were many places where I was, and if you read the interview in *Playboy* you will see that."

Kornstein said, "That was part of your process of being sensitive and understanding?"

Elliot, recognizing his opportunity, replied with unction, "There are times when a particular question must be asked, and whether it's comfortable or not truth requires that you ask it."

A few weeks before my trip to Durham, I had spoken with Elliot on the telephone. At the trial, under Bostwick's questioning, he had identified himself as a "distinguished adviser on international relations" to Mervyn Dymally, a black California congressman. He had listed black politics, civil rights, and civil liberties among the courses he taught at North Carolina Central, and the Association for the Study of Afro-American Life and History among the professional organizations he belonged to, and he had cited several black men and women—Alex Haley, Shirley Chisholm, and Julian Bond—among the subjects he had interviewed, so I had assumed that he himself was black. But on the telephone I learned that Elliot was white and Jewish. He had got into the field of black studies by accident. An early teaching job had been at the University of

Alaska, where he had been hired to teach history; when he arrived, he was told that he would be teaching a course in black studies. "I had no formal preparation in black studies, and it came to me very quickly that the faculty and administration's aim was to kill the black-studies program," he told me. "When their intent became clear to me, I determined that I would teach the course anyway, and learn as I went along. And the more I taught it and studied it, the more interested I got in it. It became clear to me that there was a lack of books in the field, and since blacks weren't writing them, I would. And when I talked to the publishers they would say, 'Well, this is a good idea, but you should know that, one, blacks don't buy books and don't read them, and, two, there is no market for black-related subject matter.' I viewed that as racist."

Elliot, when he arrived at Shedlick's office, proved to be a short, rotund man with thinning curly gray hair, a dark complexion, and thick glasses; he looked older than his age, which was forty. Although our telephone conversation had prepared me for his seriousness and earnestness, it had not prepared me for his austerity. It is rare to be in the presence of someone as grudging of himself as Elliot is; the ordinary small gestures of affability that we automatically extend to one another and automatically expect others to extend to us were not extended by Elliot. He stayed within himself, he would give no quarter, he refused every gambit of friendliness and playfulness. Shedlick and Elliot were well acquainted; Elliot's research for his book on MacDonald had brought him to Shedlick, and Shedlick had said of him, "Dr. Elliot is not one you can buffalo. He's very adroit, very probing, very factual. You can't pull the wool over his eyes. We hit it right off." After Elliot's arrival Shedlick spoke very little and listened to

Elliot with the nonchalantly pleased air of a music teacher hearing a favorite pupil give a flawless performance of a difficult composition.

I asked Elliot how he had come to be writing a book about MacDonald. He said, "After watching a film version of *Fatal Vision* on television, I had an intuitive hunch that something was wrong, and as soon as the movie was over I went to my study and wrote to Dr. MacDonald, requesting an interview. Two weeks later, I received a letter from him saying that he'd been deluged with requests for interviews and that he wanted to do only one major one, and after reviewing my résumé and the clippings and books I had sent him he had decided to grant that interview to me. I then contacted *Playboy* and they ultimately approved the project. [Elliot's interview with MacDonald appeared in the April 1986 issue.] I spent months preparing for the interview, and then spent about twenty-five hours with MacDonald in prison."

"Do you believe he's innocent?" I asked.

"My position is that, at the very least, he deserves a new trial," Elliot said. "I would never say that I believe him to be innocent beyond a shadow of a doubt. But I would say that much of the evidence that has come out post-trial and much of the evidence that was suppressed at the time of the trial would cast a very different light on Dr. MacDonald's case if presented in court, and that in all likelihood an impartial jury would reach a very different conclusion. There is no question in my mind but that his story is believable—far in excess of reasonable doubt. If I had to believe either the government's position, which I consider very flawed, or his position, where there are still some unanswered questions, I would believe his position. I would certainly not commit him to prison on the basis of the government's case."

"One would much prefer to believe that a person one is having regular dealings with—as you are having with MacDonald—is innocent. Otherwise you are in a very uncomfortable position."

"That's right. And when the idea was raised of my writing a book telling MacDonald's story, it was not a project I rushed into with great abandon. Before I would do so, I had to be persuaded that there *was* another side, and that the other side could be made credible. I was not going to make myself look foolish proclaiming MacDonald's innocence when it could not be demonstrated. You know the stories about Norman Mailer and these Eastern journalists who have interceded on behalf of various individuals in prison. I didn't want to be that kind of writer. I had to be persuaded. And I'll tell you that one of the things that most persuaded me was the package of Xeroxes of Joe McGinniss's letters that MacDonald sent me. Those letters, more than anything else, convinced me that there was another side to the story. They were so calculated, so manipulative and deceitful—and just so wrong, in terms of what McGinniss actually felt, as against what he wrote—that I had to wonder whether McGinniss had perhaps failed to tell the truth in his book. Those letters were very disturbing. I had always admired Joe McGinniss. I had used his book *The Selling of the President* in class, and to read those letters assuring MacDonald—right up to publication—that the book would exonerate him was outrageous. At the very least, they showed a stunning lack of ethics on the part of Joe McGinniss. I don't believe in situational ethics, and I certainly don't believe that journalists have to lie and misrepresent in order to get someone to work with them. Also, I think that such duplicity casts grave doubts on what is written. To me, if freedom of the press depends on the right to lie, then it's a freedom that ought not to be protected. To tell Mrs. MacDonald on the telephone, 'I won't rest until your son is acquitted,' and then to turn around and write that book—there's something about that that's very unsavory."

I asked Elliot whether he found his relationship with MacDonald different from his relationship with other subjects.

He replied, "Not really. I view this as an important project, but I don't have a deep interpersonal relationship with him. I view this as a story that deserves to be told and that may have considerable consequences. But I am not enchanted by Dr. MacDonald the man. I'm not motivated by my personal liking for him. He certainly has not seduced me. We clearly don't have the kind of relationship that he and McGinniss had. Of course, I didn't know him until he was in prison, but under no circumstances would we have run on the beach together. I'm very different in temperament and personality from Joe McGinniss. I suspect there was a closer fit between the two of them than there is between the two of us."

"How would you characterize this difference? How are you different from McGinniss?"

"I view McGinniss as part of the Eastern literati, as someone who relishes fame, someone who is adept at name-dropping, who enjoys the accoutrements of money and influence, who likes partying and lighthearted leisure activities. I view myself as a sober academic, a serious writer who writes serious things. MacDonald and McGinniss are more traditional males than I am. They are passionately interested in sports. I am more interested in serious issues, questions of public significance."

Elliot told me about his upbringing: "I grew up in Los Angeles in a typical white Jewish family, originally from Eastern Europe. My father was not one to take expensive vacations, nor did he believe in ostentatious display. He believed in the work ethic. He taught us the work ethic and the importance of saving your money, and not spending it in a flighty manner. We had the kind of family that if at dinner I said that I had seen this bug outside, my mother or my father—usually my father—would say 'Are you interested in insects? Do you want to see more?' and if I said yes, that Saturday we would be at the Museum of Natural History.

"We were very political. We worked in political campaigns, talked politics at dinner, and became involved in causes we felt were worthy of the investment of our energies. My mother and father emphasized the importance of social commitment and of righting wrongs—all those clichés spouted by others but dismissed when it comes to effort. So when I saw the wrong of the Vietnam War, as my mother and father had, it was natural for me to proceed from simply talking about it to writing about it and marching in demonstrations. It is the same with racism, sexism, et cetera. I now teach at a predominantly black university. I have had offers to teach at prestigious institutions. But I feel it is important to use whatever talents I have to try to build certain kinds of bridges. I try to be the kind of person who demonstrates—more through my actions than through my words—that not all whites are any one thing. That's what I choose to do, as opposed to the need to teach at Harvard or Yale, or other places where they don't particularly need me, where lots of professors are more than willing to go."

Beginning to feel about this paragon as Kornstein must have felt, I couldn't resist asking an unpleasant question: "Have you had offers from Harvard or Yale?"

"I never applied," Elliot said, and added, "I get routine offers from various schools."

I asked another leading question: "You talked about the decadent life style of the East Coast literati and their leisure-time activities. Do you yourself have any leisure?"

"What I do, what I derive the greatest pleasure from, is clearly my work. If I were to win a trip to Hawaii—seven days in the sand at the beach—it would be a sentence. Not long ago, I was invited to a party at the home of the then richest man in the world, Adnan Khashoggi, who had just purchased his fifty-seventh home in California. I was then doing a book on an Indian guru—a guru to the stars and to Khashoggi. I was told that Elizabeth Taylor would be at the party, and Cary Grant and Michael York. I flew there, and I was surrounded by multimillionaires and, in some cases, multibillionaires. It was an interesting experience, but not greatly so. Most of the people I spoke to were somewhat vacuous. They talked about their latest purchases or their favorite restaurants or their yachts or their latest deals. These are not the sort of things that motivate me. I don't identify with them, and I resent the decadence they represent, knowing that a third of the country lives in poverty, and that kids are dying in Ethiopia. I identify more with working-class people, who struggle to make ends meet, who are good to their families, and work hard to change things that need to be changed.

"MacDonald is not *my* role model. I don't intend to live my life according to the values he espouses. But whether I like him or dislike him is irrelevant in terms of why I pursue the case. I feel the case has implications well beyond him. If in fact the government can lie and send an innocent man to prison, then it can do the same thing to people who are less powerful and less influential and less wealthy than Dr. MacDonald."

Elliot went on to say that the piece of hubris that he—like McGinniss and others—believed responsible for Mac-Donald's downfall was an appearance he made on the Dick Cavett show in the fall of 1970, shortly after he had been cleared by the Army. On the show, he attacked the Army's Criminal Investigation Division for bungling its investigation of the crime and accusing him of it. (McGinniss, who had seen a tape of the show, told me how appalled he had been by MacDonald's performance: "The guy is sitting there laughing, making jokes on national television with Dick Cavett. He's sitting there talking about the murder of his wife and children—using this as a vehicle for celebrity. This was something that bothered me from the start. Why was he not just not reluctant to talk about it but desperate to capitalize on this tragedy and use it as a springboard to fame?") Elliot said, "When he went on the Cavett show, and named names and talked about how incompetent and stupid and bungling those Army people were, it galvanized them to move, to reopen the investigation. It was that show that led the Army to say, 'Do you mean to say that after we acquit him he goes after us?' MacDonald was his own worst enemy on that show. He was his own worst enemy in hiring Joe McGinniss, he was his own worst enemy in not insisting on seeing a draft of the book, he was his own worst enemy when he made McGinniss part of the defense team and gave him everything, just sort of hoping, on the basis of blind faith and McGinniss's letters, that McGinniss would do the right thing."

"McGinniss interprets this not as naïveté but as a kind of arrogance," I said. "He sees it as part of the pathology of narcissism."

"The simpler explanation is that this guy had no experience of authors," Elliot said. "He desperately wanted his story told, and here was this young, somewhat dashing— not to *me*—somewhat charismatic, well-known journalist coming to him. There's no question but that he was caught up in the glamour of the press and TV and that he welcomed the opportunity to go on the Dick Cavett show and stick it to the people who had stuck it to him. But he was so unpolished and so unsophisticated that he never realized that people watching the show would say, 'He doesn't sound very devastated for somebody who has just lost his wife and kids—all he's talking about is what happened to *him*.' It made people think he was cold and self-centered."

"That he should have been interested in appearing on the Cavett show at all, and that he didn't appear to be upset by the loss of his family—it does give one pause," I said.

"We can't conclude that he committed murder because he's not a very likable person. People are looking for perfection in him, and they're looking for qualities they think he ought to have had. It may well be that he doesn't possess the tenderness, sensitivity, judgment, warmth that we might wish he had. But that doesn't mean he committed three murders."

. . .

On an overcast day a few weeks later, I drove out on Long Island to see Bob Keeler in his office at *Newsday*. He is a fast-talking man in his mid-forties, with slightly receding hair and a slightly soft outline, who has an air of bracing directness and unpretentiousness. He told me that he had covered the MacDonald case for *Newsday* since 1973 and, a year or so before the criminal trial, had decided to write a book about it—"a sort of evenhanded book, not dealing exclusively with one side or the other, but a journalist's book, a balanced book." By the time of the trial, Keeler had submitted an outline and sample chapters to Doubleday, which held off giving him a contract until after the trial. Unfortunately for Keeler, when McGinniss entered the arena the publisher with whom he signed a contract was Dell, a subsidiary of Doubleday, and that finished Keeler's chances.

"You had bad luck there," I said. "If McGinniss hadn't come along—"

"No, something else would have happened," Keeler broke in. "When it comes to money, I have lousy luck. I'm not rich. I have my salary, and I make out, and I have a nice house. But I'm not the kind of person who is ever going to get rich." He continued, "Anyway, I decided I would go ahead and write my book and try to find another publisher. At the time, I thought Joe was going to write a book about Jeffrey the Tortured Innocent, and I didn't think that this should be the only book about the case, because I didn't think Jeffrey was innocent. But as time wore on I realized that my book was not going to get published—that all this effort, the dozens and dozens of hours I had put into the project, had been in vain. And when I became aware that McGinniss didn't think Jeffrey was innocent either, I began to give Joe material I had gathered on Long Island. I wanted to help out in whatever way I could, so that—I guess egotistically—I'd have some sense of participation in the book, even though it wasn't mine."

"That was very generous of you," I said.

"Well, by that time I didn't have anything to lose. I had all this information I had gathered for a purpose that no longer existed. So what was I going to do? Let it die someplace in a drawer? If the guy was writing a book that was going to be truthful, and I could help him in some small way, no big deal. Then there came a time when MacDonald, or one of MacDonald's henchpersons, sent me a bunch of McGinniss's letters to him. That's when I began to get a little ticked off at Joe. You saw what he said in the letters: 'Don't talk to Keeler.' I thought that was excessive. It was like the football Giants beating up on the Peewee football team. There was no chance I was going to get this book published. There was another thing about the letters, too—all those maudlin sentiments about 'Oh, how terrible it is that you're away, and it's such a terrible injustice.' I think McGinniss went beyond what most journalists would do in not telling Jeffrey the truth about his feelings. We could have a whole philosophical discussion here. McGinniss could say to me, 'You never told Jeffrey about your feelings, either.' That's true, I never did. In fact, one of the things about my coverage of this case that I feel good about is that I was on it for a decade and I don't think Jeffrey MacDonald ever figured out that I thought he was guilty from the first day I started writing about it. To me, that says I was writing evenhandedly and fairly. He never asked me what I thought, and I never told him what I thought, because in my view that's the way a journalist ought to behave. You ought not to be going around to people volunteering your feelings. That's daily journalism. Now, Joe was in a different situation with MacDonald: In addition to being source-and-reporter, they were business partners. So one can ask, philosophically, 'Does that change Joe's obligations to Jeffrey in terms of truth?' I don't know. I personally don't think Joe should have deceived Jeffrey."

As Keeler spoke, I could not but reflect on my own situation. As McGinniss's relationship to MacDonald had differed from the usual journalist-subject relationship in having a profit-sharing aspect, so my relationship to McGinniss was untypical because of the breach that had taken place between us so early in our acquaintance. But in all other respects—the most fundamental respects— McGinniss's enterprise with MacDonald and my enterprise with McGinniss were like all the other problematic associations of writers and subjects from which long works of nonfiction, and sometimes lawsuits, derive. In both cases, a writer had refused to accept the subject's point of view, adopting, instead, the point of view of the subject's adversaries: as McGinniss had come to see MacDonald with the eyes of the government prosecutors, so I, as I proceeded with my researches, had come to regard McGinniss with the eyes of Bostwick and his staff. I was more fortunate than McGinniss precisely because of his refusal to speak with me: by banishing me, he had freed me from the guilt I would otherwise have felt. You can't betray someone you barely know; you can only irritate and anger him and make him wish he had never made himself known to you. However, in another respect—a literary rather than a personal one—I was just as unfortunate as McGinniss. Like him, I had drawn a subject for whom I had no love and out of whom, consequently, it would be hard to fashion a literary character. I noted earlier that MacDonald was not one of the "naturals" of nonfiction who, like Perry Smith and Joe Gould, do a lot of the writer's work for him through their own special self-invention; but I omitted a crucial element of the transformation from life to literature that the masters of the nonfiction genre achieve. This is the writer's identification with and affection for the subject, without which the transformation cannot take place. The Joe Goulds and the Perry Smiths of life tend to be windy bores and pathetic nut cases; only in literature, after they have got under the skin of a writer, do they achieve the ambition of fantastic interestingness that in actuality they only grotesquely gesture toward. MacDonald had no such ambition. He insisted, and continues to insist, on his ordinariness: "I'm just this nice guy caught in a nightmare of the law, fighting for my innocence." McGinniss, if he had believed him and had written about him as innocent, would have created a more convincing, if still not deeply fascinating, character, rather than the incoherently unevil murderer he had to settle for. Similarly, if I believed in McGinniss's side of the lawsuit and could write about him as the victim of a vicious act of vengeance on the part of a disgruntled subject, I, too, could create a better character. Like McGinniss's MacDonald, my McGinniss doesn't quite add up.

"Did you feel bad about giving up the book?" I asked Keeler.

"I was disappointed. It was the first time in my life that I had a subject for a book—I felt competent, I knew the subject inside out. I honestly don't know whether my book would have sold as well as Joe's. My book would have probably been a more balanced, journalistic book, not necessarily coming to any conclusion, though I probably would have had to do that in the end. You can't dodge that bullet."

"Do you have a theory about the motive?"

"I don't think it was any one thing, but it's clear from everything Jeffrey has said, and from everything I know and from everything Joe knows, that Jeffrey's penis should go to the Smithsonian Institution when he dies. I mean, this man was extremely active sexually, extremely promiscuous, and it's not clear whether Colette became aware of that or not." Keeler went on to criticize McGinniss for not probing more deeply into MacDonald's past on Long Island, where, Keeler felt, the answer to the enigma of the man's personality lay, gleaming and waiting to be plucked. "He should have spent months there, talking to people," Keeler said. "I didn't have a chance to do that kind of reporting. I was then working eighteen hours a day as *Newsday*'s bureau chief in Albany, and could work on the book only on weekends. In fact, to be honest about it, I don't understand what Joe did with those four years he was writing the book. If you're going to be a reporter, you have to practice the craft. You have to go out and talk to people. You have to track things down. You have to talk to dozens and dozens of people." He paused, and then said, "I don't want this to sound like total sour grapes—that I'm saying all these terrible things about Joe as a journalist, and about his moral choices, just because he got his book written and I didn't. The fact is, I'm sort of bemused by the whole thing. It's typical of my luck. Here was a chance for me to make some money, and I wasn't much surprised when it didn't work out; I sort of felt in my bones that it wasn't going to work out."

As I was saying goodbye, Keeler, with his irrepressible desire to be helpful, thrust upon me a large blue loose-leaf book containing the transcripts of his interviews with Mac-Donald, McGinniss, and others for the article "Convict and Writer," which appeared in *The Newsday Magazine* on September 11, 1983. The transcripts were methodically arranged and labelled according to subject matter ("Jeff Origins," "Joe Reporting," "Joe Trial"), and were prefaced by lists of the questions Keeler planned to ask, and an outline of the text. When I got home, I leafed through the book and put it aside. I had not asked for it, and I felt there was something almost illicit about having it in my possession. To read Keeler's interviews would be like eavesdropping on someone else's conversation, and to use anything from them would be like stealing. Above all—and cutting much deeper than any concern about eavesdropping and stealing—was the affront to my pride. An interview, after all, is only as good as the journalist who conducts it, and I felt—to put it bluntly—that Keeler, with his prepared questions and his newspaper-reporter's directness, would not get from his subjects the kind of authentic responses that I try to elicit from mine with a more Japanese technique. When I finally read Keeler's transcripts, however, I was in for a surprise and an illumination. MacDonald and McGinniss had said exactly the same things to the unsubtle Keeler that they had said to me. It hadn't made the slightest difference that Keeler had read from a list of prepared questions and I had acted as if I were passing the time of day. From Keeler's blue book I learned the same truth about subjects that the analyst learns about patients: they will tell their story to anyone who will listen to it, and the story will not be affected by the behavior or personality of the listener; just as ("good enough") analysts are interchangeable, so are journalists. My McGinniss and Keeler's McGinniss were the same person, and so were my MacDonald and Keeler's MacDonald and McGinniss's MacDonald. The subject, like the patient, dominates the relationship and calls the shots. The journalist cannot create his subjects any more than the analyst can create his patients. A few weeks after the settlement of the McGinniss lawsuit, MacDonald sent out a jubilant message to his followers in the *MacDonald Defense Update*, an irregularly published newsletter put out by MacDonald's out-of-prison "liaison" volunteer worker, Gail Boyce, in which he exhibited the very quality—a sort of reflexive and unremitting bogusness—that he most sought to repudiate in McGinniss's characterization. The message read, in part:

> The trial proved to all neutral observers that *Fatal Vision* is a fiction book masquerading as non-fiction. . . . Since we have proven his lies, since we have the truth now in the transcripts of a Federal Court proceeding, and since he was desperate enough to settle to offer the amount that was finally accepted, I felt it was proper to accept this victory and move on. . . .
>
> Truthfully, working so intensely in and around the sordid lies of McGinniss's book and hearing his pathetic attempts at justifying his actions by calling in highly paid witnesses to make outrageous statements, is simply an awful experience. Not only did I personally feel it was best to move on to more positive and meaningful projects, but my family, *all* the attorneys involved in the defense, and our excellent defense team *all* agreed it was an opportune time to return to the criminal investigation itself and the procedures we are undertaking to eventually win my vindication.

In my talks and correspondence with MacDonald I glimpsed some of the more appealing facets of his

—for example, his stoicism in the face of the
conditions of solitary confinement—and I came
to allow for the vapidity of his speech and writing, as one
allows for a handicap. But the MacDonald of *Fatal Vision*
was also there. McGinniss betrayed him and devastated him and possibly misjudged him, but he didn't
invent him.

WHEN I walked into Daniel Kornstein's office in mid-
Manhattan, a week after the settlement, he said,
"Didn't you get my message? I called to cancel this ap-
pointment." I looked at him innocently. Two days earlier,
he had agreed to see me, and almost immediately had
repented of it, leaving a message on my answering machine cancelling the meeting. Inspired by Keeler's lecture
on the necessity for reporters to report, I decided to ignore
the message, and turned up in Kornstein's office at the
appointed hour. He wearily accepted my presence and
immediately declared, "McGinniss and I are not going to
talk about the case or coöperate on it." He was a pained-
looking, short, dark-haired youngish man.

"You sent me that letter," I said.

"When we wrote the letter, we wanted to alert the media and make people aware of the new doctrine being
advocated," Kornstein said. "The case is over as far as we
are concerned. Everything we want to say is in the transcript. Particularly the cross-examination of MacDonald
and my summation. These were the key moments of the
trial. We think the public record speaks for itself. I try my
cases in the courtroom."

"Then why did you send out that letter?" I asked.

Kornstein gestured helplessly. "I'm sorry. I can't answer you." Then he said, "The judge in the case didn't see—was blind to—the First Amendment implications of the case. He is a new federal judge, appointed in 1984. He had been a state judge for sixteen years. He once played professional baseball—the Chicago Cubs were interested in him."

I asked a question about the trial, and Kornstein again said, "I'm sorry. I can't answer you." He added, "We are trying to put the case behind us."

"Would you rather I didn't write about it?" I asked.

"I would never want to say I would rather that something were not written," Kornstein said piously.

I asked him if his offer to let me read documents in his office—an offer made before McGinniss broke off relations with me—still held. "It's a matter of convenience for me," I said. "Your office is a few blocks from where I live, and Bostwick's office is three thousand miles away."

Kornstein said he would consider my request and let me know. Suddenly, he said, "Do you know anything about me?"

I looked at him with interest, and thought, Now all will be explained. This is going to be one of those moments of revelation, when the beggar discloses that he is the prince.

"I am Vanessa Redgrave's lawyer," Kornstein said. "I represented her in her suit against the Boston Symphony."

It was time to go. "Will you let me know if I can read those trial documents here?" I asked. "I'll give you my phone number."

"No, no, I have it," Kornstein said, shuffling through papers on his desk. "I have dozens of pieces of paper with your phone number on them. I know your number by heart"—and then, bitterly, comically, he recited it. He presented me with two books he had written (*Thinking*

Under Fire: Great Courtroom Lawyers and Their Impact on American History and *The Music of the Laws*) and politely escorted me to the door. I never heard from him again.

"Did you ask Bostwick if he took the case on contingency?" Joseph Wambaugh said to me when I called him at his house in San Marino. "You can depend on it that he did." Before I could tell him he was wrong, he went on, "You can bet the bank on it. Otherwise, it wouldn't have got as far as it did. I myself have been sued so many times that it doesn't matter whether it's Mr. Bostwick or somebody else; it's always the same. You could confer with every attorney in town, and you could draft the most binding, airtight, rock-solid legal release in the world, and the subject would sign it—and you could still find yourself in court, because any imaginative, resourceful lawyer can dream up a cause of action and bring a lawsuit. What does he have to lose? In Britain, if someone brings a libel action he runs a certain risk, because if he doesn't prevail he has to pay the defendant's legal fees. Here the plaintiff risks nothing, and once the mechanism of the suit is in motion the defendant is going to suffer—and I mean suffer. He immediately starts hemorrhaging his hard-earned bucks. Very few people have the stamina to endure one of these lawsuits. To defend himself, McGinniss had to come out here and live in a hotel for six weeks. He has a young child, he has a young family, he has a life as a college professor, he's trying to write a book. He gave all that up for the principle of coming out here in defense. The MacDonald side would have settled; they would have settled for the same amount early on. McGinniss refused as a matter of principle. But when he came out here and got ground up in the system and dragged through it and saw what it was really about—it's about the contingency system—he said, 'Principle is principle, but this is really killing me.' I saw McGinniss toward the end. He looked ten years older. I assure you, when you're the victim of one of these lawsuits you are awake at three a.m. even if you don't drink. You're awake with the boozers, going crazy with homicidal impulses. My first nonfiction book, *The Onion Field*, brought me three lawsuits. One of them lasted twelve years. Think of that. Children grow up. Think of how many nights I saw at three a.m. At that time, publishers didn't have insurance policies, the way they do now. Guess who paid for that lawsuit. My publisher and I split it down the middle. These contingency lawyers—they're like garden slugs and boll weevils. You can't get rid of them. Where is Agent Orange when we really need it? These guys are everywhere. We have twenty-five thousand lawyers in L.A. County. If we adopted the British system, all these contingency lawyers that keep spewing out of our law schools would have to go do something else they're qualified for, like selling aluminum siding in Indiana or Veg-O-Matics on TV."

I asked Wambaugh what his experience of testifying at the trial had been.

"It was a joke," he said, and went on, "The question that some of the jurors made such a big deal of was 'Have you ever lied to the subject of a book?' The answer is no. But I haven't always told the truth. I've dealt with sociopaths, murderers, other horrible people—as a cop and as a writer—and by no means would I always tell them the truth, though I wouldn't lie to them. What's the difference between a lie and an untruth? Simple. With a lie, there's malice involved, there's ill will. With an untruth, there isn't. You go to a thirty-year reunion and everybody in the room is telling untruths. Everybody. 'Oh, how great you look!' That sort of thing. When I'm talking to a sociopath, a killer—either as a cop or as a writer—and the guy says, 'You can identify with the feelings I had when I raped those thirteen women, can't you? You know how I felt, and you would have done the same thing, wouldn't you?,' I'll say, 'Oh, sure, Charlie. Hell, I can't quit smoking or drinking, so how can I criticize you? Have another candy bar.' *Of course* that's what I'll say, to keep the guy talking. But there is no malice involved. Now, if I said, 'Charlie, if you confess to those thirteen rapes I'll see to it that the D.A. drops all charges and lets you plead a parking ticket'—that's illegal, there's ill will and malice there, and *that's a lie*. This is what I tried to explain to the jury. Well, look, let's talk about juries. Does one get a jury of one's peers? If there had been a chance of Joe McGinniss getting a jury of his peers, Bostwick would never have filed a complaint. Joe McGinniss got an average big-city jury, which is what Bostwick knew he'd get. On the entire jury panel there was one person who was a college graduate. Bostwick got rid of that sucker immediately in his peremptory challenges. One of the jurors testified that she'd read maybe one book in her life. When I sat there and looked at those people, I started sweating for McGinniss. His peers—people of similar background and education—don't get on juries. The jurors, almost one and all, said afterward that they didn't understand writers, they didn't understand the publishing world, they didn't understand anything that Buckley and Wambaugh were saying up there, they didn't understand this business of the difference between a lie and an untruth. They said there's no difference, and if you tell somebody anything that isn't exactly true you should be punished for it. One person said she wanted to give MacDonald millions and millions of dollars. I tell you, people who were McGinniss's equals in education, background, and experience wouldn't have responded like that. He did not get a jury of his peers, and he would never get one. He knew that. Would he want to go through that again, for the principle, for all writers everywhere? Well, no. He finally said, 'Screw it. Let's settle.' And I don't blame him a bit. I'm sorry about it. It makes me sick—it makes me absolutely sick—to think that that psychopathic baby-killer will get three hundred and twenty-five thousand dollars out of that. It makes me want to puke."

"I know there was a lot of criticism of your testimony among the jurors," I said.

"Oh, absolutely. I was sitting there talking to people who have never read a book, some of them. I might as well have been speaking Chinese when I talked about the difference between a lie and an untruth in an interview with a sociopathic killer. I knew they didn't understand me, and I wasn't surprised at their reactions. When you talk to a sociopathic criminal, you have to flatter him and curry favor with him by telling him something that isn't absolutely true. You have no choice but to do it, whether you're a police officer or a writer. They *will* put you in that position. They do it. They enjoy it. They'll say 'You do believe me, don't you?' right at a point where you're convinced they're lying. If you say no, you could lose everything you've gained, including your book, your money, your time if you're a writer, and your case if you're a cop. So you cannot tell the truth."

"Well, I guess everybody has to decide that one for himself—and you've decided it this way. But that's not the only way a person could decide."

"What would you do? Would you lose everything?"

"I know it's very easy to put on moral airs and to say 'I would have behaved—' "

"No, I want you to put on moral airs. I want you to see where the morality lies. I want you to see that as a cop I had a moral obligation to the people of Los Angeles to make this case, and if by telling an untruth—not a lie—to a sociopathic criminal I could better protect the people of L.A., then I had a moral obligation to the people to do it. Put me in the position of the writer—I tried to tell them this at the trial. I said, 'A book is a living thing. When you get to the point where you have this entire investment in it, then this book is as much alive as anyone you've ever known—sometimes more so—and you have a moral obligation to protect that life, to not let it die aborning. If I have to tell an untruth to a sociopathic criminal to protect this living thing, to let it be born, then that's where my moral obligation lies.' "

The next day, Wambaugh called me. He said there was something he wanted to talk about: he felt dissatisfied with the end of our conversation, when he had pressed me to say that I, too, regarded the books I had written as living things, and I had felt obliged to say that I didn't. "I guess I felt silly after talking to you about that," he said disarmingly. "It's something I just never questioned. I always assumed that every writer felt this way about his work. I've read hundreds of writers who say that in the course of writing a book the story takes over and the characters take over and it's almost as if they themselves were not involved."

I said, "It has been said of characters in novels that they seem more real than people in life—"

"Yes, yes," Wambaugh cut in. "And they seem to do things of their own volition, without any help from you."

"But that's *fiction*. In nonfiction, which is what you and I and McGinniss write, the characters don't need to 'take on a life of their own.' They already have one in actuality."

"I know," said Wambaugh. "But I write it in the style of a novel. I write what Truman Capote called 'the non-fiction novel.' "

I already knew about Wambaugh's writing techniques from his testimony at the MacDonald-McGinniss trial. In answer to Kornstein's questioning, Wambaugh had said,

> When I write non-fiction, obviously I was not there when the events occurred. I write in a dramatic style—that is, I employ lots of dialogue, I describe feelings, I describe how the events must have taken place. I invent probable dialogue or at least possible dialogue based upon all of the research that I do. . . . And in order to have the artistic freedom I need, I get a legal release whenever I can.

Wambaugh returned to the book-as-living-thing theme. "I used to think of books as living things, corny as it sounds, even before I began to write. I felt *Call of the Wild* was a living thing, and then *Moby Dick*."

"What about boring books?" I asked. "Are they living things?"

"No. They don't come alive for me. But I'm sure that the authors of those books go to their graves thinking they have brought something to life. And maybe people don't feel that I have brought something to life, but I feel that I have. I'm not an intellectual. I write from the guts, and I'm talking to you from the same part of my anatomy. When I was testifying, Bostwick tried to make a book seem like a pair of shoes. I said that when I wrote my first book I didn't have a thought about making money; I only thought what a great honor it would be to get something published. Even now, I don't write for money. I've made plenty of money. I don't even think about money anymore, except when I have to pay lawyers who are trying to bankrupt me."

"So you're one of those lucky people who write for the pleasure of it, and who happened to strike a nerve that has caused millions of people to buy your books."

"That's right. I feel it's a goddam miracle. And because I've been blessed like this, and had this enormous stroke of luck, I feel I have an obligation, as McGinniss felt he had one, to fight for those other authors, ninety-nine per cent of whom can't even think of making a living from writing."

ON SEPTEMBER 18, 1987, McGinniss appeared on William F. Buckley's television talk show "Firing Line," together with Floyd Abrams, the New York libel lawyer and expert on the First Amendment. Watching a tape of the program a few months later, I was fascinated by the transformation McGinniss had undergone. The defensive and uncomfortable man I had spoken with in Williamstown and the desperate, hounded, Orestes-like figure of the trial transcript had become a relaxed and expansive celebrity author, exuding a kind of boyish excitement and disbelief about being somebody in the world. I had met this McGinniss, too, in the letters to MacDonald; showing off his worldly successes to MacDonald was evidently as deep a need for him as was misleading MacDonald about the book. "*The New York Times Book Review* is not only going to do a major review [of *Going to Extremes*] but is actually sending someone up here next week to interview me," McGinniss wrote happily to MacDonald in a letter of August 6, 1980. "That is like having Knighthood conferred." On July 16, 1982, he boasted to MacDonald about Phyllis Grann, his new editor at Putnam (McGinniss had changed publishers by this time), who was "probably the highest-ranking, most prestigious and successful woman in the entire publishing business" (even though, as McGinniss felt constrained to let MacDonald know, she "started in publishing as Nelson Doubleday's secretary"). Five months later, he triumphantly described to MacDonald, in his cell, the sales conference at which *Fatal Vision* had been presented: "At the conclusion of the presentation of this book, which consisted of not only Phyllis Grann raving about it but marketing director, book-club & subsidiary-rights person, publicity director, and finally the president of the company all saying how special it was . . . sales reps were asked to conduct a secret ballot to rate the books in terms of how they thought they would sell—and *Fatal Vision* (and this is a secret, please, no Xeroxes of this letter to friends in Cal. or anywhere else!)—was chosen *number one*."

Now, on television, sitting with people who were clearly on his side, McGinniss chatted easily and fluently about the lawsuit, like a man recounting to a dinner table of friends a freakish misfortune that had befallen him on his way to work. After listening to McGinniss's account, Abrams remarked, "One of the startling things to me is that here you have someone who the [criminal-trial] jury has found committed this most heinous of all acts, and you still had people on the [civil-trial] jury who listened with great interest, maybe sympathy, and willingness to treat him like everyone else. Maybe a jury is supposed to do that, but it's pretty unusual when you have a murderer in front of you." The dialogue continued:

McGINNISS: As one of them put it to me afterward—we were permitted, and indeed encouraged, to speak to the jurors after the non-verdict was reached—
BUCKLEY: Including Dr. MacDonald?
McGINNISS: No, he wasn't. His lawyers were, but he himself was reincarcerated at that time. He was present during the trial. He was in court all day, dressed like this in suits, no handcuffs on, in the presence of the jury, which was like a summer vacation for him. It was great, you know—you get out of jail. But at the end, one of the jurors said to me, "The fact, Mr. McGinniss, is that it wasn't MacDonald who was on trial here. It was you. You were the defendant. You were the one we had to judge."

Buckley led the discussion to the issue on which he himself had testified:

BUCKLEY: Let me ask you this, Mr. Abrams. Suppose [McGinniss] had said, responding truthfully in all matters, "I absolutely knew he was guilty on the first of April, 1975, but I continued to let him think that I thought he was innocent for two years." Would that have justified a finding for the plaintiff?
ABRAMS: I don't believe so. I really don't. I mean, that raises a nice issue of the difference between the sort of situations which the law ought to deal with and the sort of situations which allow us to pass a moral judgment on

somebody but which the law, as such, is not designed to deal with.

BUCKLEY: You have had a lot of dealings with the press. Was I incorrect in testifying, as I did, that a writer—especially an investigative writer—very often gives an impression intending to disarm the person he's writing about? Does that shock you ethically or in any other sense?

ABRAMS: No, it doesn't. But I will tell you that I have interviewed a lot of jurors, and any sort of action by journalists which misleads people is something that a lot of ordinary citizens—non-lawyers, non-journalists—find very offensive.

McGinniss told Buckley and Abrams how the mistrial had come about: "After three days of deliberation, the jury expressed the view that they were hopelessly—not even deadlocked so much as confused—and were not going to be able to render a verdict. . . . There was a special verdict form which had thirty-seven different boxes to check off 'Yes' or 'No,' and it became apparent that they simply didn't understand how the facts that had been presented at the trial related to the questions that they had in front of them, and after three days they announced that they were unable to really agree upon anything, and they asked to be allowed to go home."

THE jurors themselves told a different story about the mistrial. When I met with four of them in Los Angeles, they said they had felt capable of making their way through the verdict form (two of the six jurors held master's degrees), but were helpless in the face of a juror named Lucille Dillon, who refused to deliberate. After the first question on the verdict form had been discussed and voted on, with five in favor of MacDonald and one, Dillon, in favor of McGinniss, Dillon walked away from the table and would have nothing further to do with the group, sitting near a window reading, while the rest, perforce, deliberated on what to do about her. "Our mistake was that when we wrote a letter to the judge telling him that Lucille wouldn't deliberate, we said she was for McGinniss," Sheila Campbell told me. "If we had left it open, and just said we were having trouble with Lucille, we might have got another juror in." This was so. When the judge proposed to Bostwick and Kornstein that Dillon be replaced with an alternate, Kornstein naturally refused to relinquish a juror known to be on his side, and the judge was forced to declare a mistrial. The trouble had started early in the trial, when Dillon, an animal-rights activist, brought animal-rights literature to the jury room and wasn't able to interest the other jurors in her cause. She became the weird Other to the majority, and they became the Oppressors to her. When the time for deliberations came, the majority realized too late— like other majorities who have ignored the warning signals of annoying minorities—that they had scorned this woman at their peril and were now powerless against her.

I spent the afternoon of Thanksgiving, 1987, with Lucille Dillon in my hotel room in Los Angeles. She was a pleasant-looking, self-possessed woman of sixty, with graying curly hair, who was wearing white slacks, a white overblouse, and white sneakers on very tiny feet; she spoke in a melodious soft voice and had a most appealing deep-throated chuckle. We ate a room-service lunch of avocado salad and sherbet, and she told me of her experiences at the trial.

"I saw McGinniss as a very good man," she said. "It just showed about him. We've all met people where we get this strong impression of goodness. MacDonald? I had no feeling one way or the other about him. I wondered about him, but I had no impression of him. I liked both the lawyers. They both looked like very good men, too, and I thought they did very good jobs. There was something about them, the look in their eyes, something good. I thought the judge was a very nice man, very patient, kindly, courteous, considerate."

I said, "The defense has criticized the judge for letting the case come to trial. They said that he didn't understand that this was a First Amendment case, and that if he had he would have dismissed it."

"I agree with that. To me, the First Amendment was on trial in this case—the First Amendment of the Constitution, guaranteeing the right to free speech. I saw that very early. I understood that someone was trying to stop someone from saying something, and I didn't like it one bit. I believe in the Constitution."

"When did you develop your interest in the First Amendment?"

"In high school, I read the Constitution, and I loved it. It was a wonderful thing to read, just beautiful. It protected people. This was a document that protected you, and they would have to fight against that document to get to you unfairly. On a trip to Washington, I got a copy of the Constitution. I haven't read it all. I tried to. I read most of it, but it got a little tedious, and I quit. I just totally believe in it. It's not always enforced, it's not always used by the government. This is a complaint I have. There are many unconstitutional things the government does."

"What things are you thinking of?"

"I'm thinking of the income tax. One of the reasons the Constitution was written was to guarantee that Congress control the money supply, and that it not get into the private hands of bankers. The federal income tax was put into effect in 1913—even though the Constitution forbids that—and now people don't have much of anything. Everything is taxed."

Dillon told me that she had remarried her second husband after being divorced from him for nineteen years. "It's really a financial arrangement," she said. "I said to him, 'I'm getting on in years, and if anything should happen to you the boys will be stuck taking care of me. There aren't too many jobs in Oxnard.' That is where I was at the time. I did odd jobs, I worked at the Fabric Well awhile, little things, but they don't last, those kinds of jobs. So I said, 'Why don't you marry me again, so I can have your Social Security? In case anything happens, the boys won't have to take care of Mother in her old age.' He said, 'I'll think about it,' and then he said O.K. So he has his life—his quiet life—and I have mine. He has his room, and I have my room. We own a mobile home together. It was strictly a money deal. Strange, isn't it?"

As I listened to Lucille Dillon, I felt more acutely conscious than ever of the surrealism that is at the heart of journalism. People tell journalists their stories as characters in dreams deliver their elliptical messages: without warning, without context, without concern for how odd they will sound when the dreamer awakens and repeats them. Here I sat, eating my Thanksgiving dinner with this stranger dressed in white, whom I would never see again, and whose existence for me henceforth would be on paper, as a sort of emblematic figure of the perils of the jury system.

"Was it Kornstein who persuaded you?" I asked.

"Oh, no. Nothing persuaded me. As more information came out, it just confirmed me more and more. Everything that was said as the case unfolded confirmed what I knew at the beginning. I could not change my mind."

Dillon went on to speak of her aversion to the other jurors. "I felt something was going on that wasn't right. I wondered, Are these people supporters of MacDonald? Could it be that everyone in this room is a MacDonald supporter? How come they're so sympathetic to him? I wondered about that. I will always wonder about that. They got along with each other beautifully. It was as if they had already known each other, they were so friendly. They laughed all the time, and talked constantly and loud, and they were all of one mind, like one person, in full agreement. They were not very intelligent. I'm not saying that I am, but I sensed a lack of intelligence in these people. They were childish and silly and ignorant. It's not nice to be around people like that. I went into the hall a few times to get away from them, from their nasty dispositions and nasty attitudes. I was on a jury a few years ago, and it was the same. They were not nice people. It was a trial about a young man. They were going to hang that young man for a questionable thing. The boy was accused of smuggling marijuana into prison. They wanted to send him to prison. They were older folks. They were mean. They didn't care if they ruined his life. I couldn't agree to it."

"So it was another hung jury?"

"It was another hung jury."

McGinniss, in one of his late letters to MacDonald, quoted a passage he had written earlier in the day which he evidently felt it safe to let MacDonald read (though "I'm bending my principles even to do this"), about the criminal-trial judge's attitude toward Bernard Segal, MacDonald's defense counsel:

> Judge Dupree was possessed of an unusually mobile, expressive face, and, from the earliest days of the trial, the expression most often seen upon it, as Bernie Segal conducted cross-examination, was one of distaste. Obviously alert, attentive, and sometimes even taking notes during Blackburn's direct examination, the judge would lean back in his chair with his eyes closed, grimacing in exasperation or rubbing his temples as if his head ached, during those periods when Segal was aggressively questioning a prosecution witness.

I thought of this passage when I met Segal in San Francisco, where he practices law and is a professor at the Golden Gate University School of Law. He is a round, extremely voluble man of sixty, with a head of curly gray hair, who seems caught in a perpetual struggle between his sense of himself as a serious and dignified person and an antic force within him bent on subverting this self-image. He said, "It was my idea from the outset to have a writer in our midst. Having spent some time as a journalist before I went honest and became a lawyer, I thought, There aren't many books written from the inside of a case, and this is a unique case with a unique client. A lot of the time, you're embarrassed by your client in a criminal case.

Not because your client is necessarily guilty but because, generally speaking, people are not dragged into criminal cases for no reason. There's usually something about their conduct that is a little off, that makes them vulnerable to the charge. So as a lawyer you say, 'My God, I don't want a reporter hanging around and seeing this side of my client—we'd better not let him in with us.' Jeff MacDonald was one in a million, as a client and as a human being, and I thought, Here we have a real person, someone the reader will identify with. Jeff MacDonald doesn't look like and is not like the average criminal defendant. This is a three-dimensional, warm, caring, decent human being caught up in a nightmare of the law. He was for me an American Dreyfus. The story of Dreyfus was one my father made me read as a child. He took me to see the Paul Muni movie of the Zola story. I lived it a hundred times."

Segal went on to speak bitterly of Judge Dupree's ruling that psychiatric evidence would not be admissible at the trial. The defense had planned to introduce the testimony of several psychiatrists who had examined MacDonald— both at the time of the murders and at the time of the criminal trial—and had found him sane and unlikely to have committed the crimes. As Michael Malley later recalled, at the McGinniss trial, "The prosecution had announced, 'If we prove that this man did it, we don't have to prove why he did it or that he's the kind of man who could have done it.' We thought that was a very unsatisfying view of life to give to a jury, and we were going to spend a lot of time, if the judge would let us, trying to prove what kind of man Jeff MacDonald was, to prove that he was not the kind of man who could have done it." Here, as in several other places in the McGinniss trial, what was not supposed to happen—the trial was not supposed to be a retrial of MacDonald—did in fact happen. In the course of challenging the fairness of McGinniss's book (using Segal's "essential integrity" clause as his shaky justification), Bostwick also succeeded in raising the issue of the fairness of the criminal trial. In his examinations of Malley, Segal, and MacDonald, he bore down heavily on an incident that had preceded Judge Dupree's ruling on the psychiatric testimony. At first, the judge had been disposed to consider allowing the defense its psychiatrists—provided that the prosecution be allowed to have a go at MacDonald with a psychiatrist of its own choosing. MacDonald reluctantly agreed to submit to an examination by the enemy's psychiatrist, a Dr. James A. Brussel, of New York, who came to Raleigh accompanied by a clinical psychologist from West Orange, New Jersey, named Hirsch Lazaar Silverman. The examination of MacDonald took place on the evening of August 13, 1979, in an attorney's office, and at the McGinniss trial Segal testified about a less than encouraging encounter he had had with Brussel after it was over:

Dr. Brussel was standing there in the waiting room. He was dressed in a suit and he had a hat on. And when I came in, I said something about, "Well, I'm glad it's all done already," and Dr. Brussel said, "Where's my hat?" I was sort of taken aback. I thought perhaps he was jesting. But he was a man close to eighty years of age and I realized he really wasn't kidding. And we all sort of looked a little bit startled, and he was turning around looking for his hat, and finally someone said, "Dr. Brussel, your hat's on your head." He said, "Oh, yes." Then he said, "Where am I? What place is this?" And we again were a little bit taken aback . . . and finally one of us said, "Dr. Brussel, this is

Raleigh, North Carolina." He said, "Oh yes—yes, of course."

After the judge received Brussel and Silverman's evaluation of MacDonald, he ruled against admitting any psychiatric testimony from either side: "To pit shrink versus shrink would simply tend to prolong the case and at best would prove something that would just tend to confuse the issues." In the McGinniss trial, Bostwick asked MacDonald, "Did Mr. McGinniss say anything to you about the judge's decision not to allow psychiatric testimony?" MacDonald replied, "He said it was outrageous."

"Did he say why?"

"Yes, because he said he was—he was referring to Brussel—a senile, incompetent son of a bitch."

However, when he came to write *Fatal Vision*, McGinniss—probably because he was struggling to lend substance to his portrait of MacDonald as a psychopath— quoted at length from the Brussel-Silverman report, which reads like the work of a parodist, as in "There seems to be an absence in him of deep emotional response, coupled with an inability to profit from experience. He is the kind of individual who is subject to committing asocial acts with impunity." And "In terms of mental health and personality functioning, he is either an overt or a repressed sexual invert characterized by expansive egotism and delusions of persecution. He is preoccupied with the irrelevant and is unable to face reality."

Unknown to MacDonald and his lawyers until many years later, when the Freedom of Information Act led to the discovery, Dr. Brussel was not merely a fragile old man at the end of his career; he was a forensic psychiatrist who in 1971 had assisted the government in mounting its case against MacDonald, and who had advanced the theory that MacDonald killed Colette during an argument, and then killed the children because they were witnesses. "There is no question that the prosecution pulled a fast one when they selected him as the psychiatrist to give MacDonald what was supposed to be a neutral psychiatric examination," Segal told me. "We got lumped by the judge in a ferocious manner. I've never seen a case like this in the twenty-seven years I've been practicing. Jeff could in fact be guilty, but when a man is convicted at a ruthless, unfair trial, the system is violated, and everyone is less safe. Having said that, however, I know, as well as anybody can know who was not there on February 17, 1970, that he didn't do it."

IN FEBRUARY of 1988, I paid a second visit to MacDonald at Terminal Island. He was to have been returned to his old prison in Arizona after the settlement of the McGinniss lawsuit but had formally requested to be allowed to remain at Terminal Island in order to be close to his ill mother, who lives in nearby Long Beach. The request was granted on the condition that he continue in solitary confinement, and he accepted the condition. We sat in the same visitors' room, after he had gone through the same ritual with the handcuffs, and I asked him about one of McGinniss's letters which had made a strong impression on me—as much because of what MacDonald had done to the letter as because of what McGinniss had written: MacDonald had taken a pen and had, as it were, vandalized the letter, covering each of its seven pages with a variety of savage marks. The letter's entire text had been crossed out, paragraph by paragraph, as if by someone striking blows at the defenseless words on the page. When I first saw the letter, I felt in the presence of a terrible anger and hatred and desire to do injury. For me, it was, and remains, the only sign of anything disturbing and uncanny about MacDonald, of anything that isn't blandly "normal."

MacDonald told me that he had marked up the letter while making a tape in response to the questions McGinniss asked in it. "I was so angry about having to make the tape that each time I answered a question I'd cross it out with my pen like that. As I'm making the tape, I'm thinking, There, you son of a bitch! You're pleading for it, and, O.K., I'll give it to you, since I have your assurances that this is just between you and me."

In the letter, more persistently than ever before, McGinniss was attempting to break through MacDonald's elusive blandness, interrogating him closely about the intimacies of his marriage. As McGinniss later testified under Bostwick's questioning, "I was trying to urge him to stop talking platitudes and start talking like a real person. . . . What he had told me up until then seemed so superficial and so lacking in genuine emotional content that I felt it wasn't all there was—there must be more, there must be things he was holding back." So McGinniss did what we all do—made the mistake we all make—when faced with a stubbornly enigmatic Other: he fell back on himself and his own experiences to solve the enigma. He wrote to MacDonald:

> I know you are an optimist, and I know you tend to block unhappy memories, but, Jeff, let's face it, early marriage is no picnic for anyone. It sure as hell wasn't for me. Marrying at twenty-one, having a child the next year, then

another in another year and a half, and then me falling in love with someone else while my wife was pregnant yet a third time. . . .

Having gone through that sort of experience myself, I think I might be more attuned than most people to the possibility that you shared some of those reactions in your own life. . . . There is enough already known in terms of your extracurricular life to demonstrate that you were at least as promiscuous as I was.

But MacDonald would not accept the gambit, would not accede to the suggestion that he and McGinniss were peas in a pod who had both wronged the dull women they had got stuck marrying. As I noted earlier, most people don't make good subjects for journalists; Mac-Donald was a member of the unpromising majority rather than of the special, auto-novelized minority. When McGinniss said he was trying to get MacDonald to "start talking like a real person," he could only have meant that he wanted him to start talking like a character in a novel. McGinniss's letter—whose object was precisely to invalidate MacDonald's reality and enlist his aid in creating a literary character out of himself—lays bare one of the fundamental differences between literary characters and people in life: literary characters are drawn with much broader and blunter strokes, are much simpler, more generic (or, as they used to say, mythic) creatures than real people, and their preternatural vividness derives from their unambiguous fixity and consistency. Real people seem relatively uninteresting in comparison, because they are so much more complex, ambiguous, unpredictable, and particular than people in novels. The therapy of psychoanalysis attempts to restore to the neurotic patient the freedom to be uninteresting that he lost somewhere along the way. It proposes to undermine the novelistic structures on which he has constructed his existence, and to destroy the web of elaborate, artful patterns in which he is caught. There are people (psychoanalysts among them) who think that the action of psychoanalysis is, as it were, to transfer the patient from one novel to another—from a gothic romance, say, to a domestic comedy—but most analysts and most people who have undergone the therapy know that this is not so, and that the Freudian program is a far more radical one. Patients in analysis sometimes say they feel they are being driven crazy by the treatment. It is the denovelization of their lives, and their glimpse into the abyss of unmediated individuality and idiosyncrasy that is the Freudian unconscious, which causes them to feel this way.

MacDonald continued to talk about McGinniss's letter: "He kept saying 'It's background' when I asked him why he wanted to discuss intimate scenes between me and a woman. I talked to him on the phone and said, 'Joe, this is crazy. This doesn't make any sense. What does this have to do with the story about the case?,' and he'd say, 'Nothing. What it does is it teaches me. I'm the artist. I have to know everything. I have to know what your sweat smells like. I want to know how you and Colette made love. Then I can choose from that. I, as the artist, have to have all this background so that I can write the true story of Jeff MacDonald, decent man in prison.' And that made sense to me, quite honestly. I think I understood what he was saying. I had made a decision—catastrophic, it turned out—to trust Joe. It turned out I was unbelievably off base. He dragged the stuff out of me, and then turned it around in the book and said, 'Here's this callous, superficial, chauvinistic, nasty human being talking about the woman he says he loves.' But that's not me. That's not my life style."

"But did you *have* to tell him those things?" I asked.

"I know, I know," MacDonald said. "And the answer—and it's not even an excuse anymore, because I'm so ashamed that I did it—is that he said he was writing a book that would get the truth out about this horrible misprosecution, and I was willing to pay the price."

As we talked, MacDonald, who had forgone his lunch to be with me, ate some small powdered-sugar doughnuts from a package I had bought at a machine in the prison-staff lunchroom, and once again I was struck by the physical grace of the man. He handled the doughnuts—breaking off pieces and unaccountably keeping the powdered sugar under control—with the delicate dexterity of a veterinarian fixing a broken wing. When the package was empty, he neatly folded it, and spoke of the abusive letters he had received by the hundred from readers of *Fatal Vision*. "There's one I'll never forget," he said. "I wake up occasionally and think of it. A guy wrote me and said, 'I'm sitting on the beach in front of the Sheraton Waikiki Hotel, and my wife and I have just read *Fatal Vision*.' Then he speaks of me as though I'm a psychotic monster. It's an unbelievably tormenting thing. Here is this guy, sitting on a beach with his wife, supposedly having a vacation, writing a vicious, hateful letter to someone in prison." I had read this letter in Bostwick's office, and I, too, had found it unbelievable. This is the letter:

August 19, 1984

Dear Inmate MacDonald,

My wife and I are here in beautiful and sunny Hawaii having a great time, and we both have read the novel *Fatal Vision* by Joe McGinniss while laying on the beach here at Waikiki.

We are both, I must tell you, convinced beyond a shadow of a doubt that you are guilty as all hell of the murders of your wife and daughters.

We have two lovely and bright daughters of our own and thank God they were not subjected to a "madman" for a father.

I have no compassion for an individual as sick, demented and sordid as surely you must be. From the text of McGinniss's well versed story about you, it is plain to see that you are a liar of outrageous stature.

Anyone who could do what he did to a pregnant woman is really a slime, but what you did to two helpless children is even sicker and more difficult to comprehend and believe. It states in the book (I believe) that you are eligible for parole in 1991. We only pray to God that the authorities in charge of such proceedings will have better sense than your Army peers did years ago and *never* let you loose. You are obviously a latent homosexual (or perhaps no longer *latent* now that you are where you are! Perhaps, by now, you may well be the "Queen of the Hop" there in the joint, hm?) who hates women because you are an impotent faggot, true?

At any rate, we just wanted you to know we enjoyed the novel but feel sure you are guilty and a pervert maniac like you should never be cut loose. You should, probably, concentrate on getting yourself a "daddy" there in the joint and becoming the true fag you really must be.

With best wishes.

J—— H——

I said, "There is something baffling and confusing to me about this. These people lying on the beach in Hawaii are writing a letter to a person they have read about in a book—to a character in a book whom you reject as a representation of yourself—and yet the letter arrives in your hands, you read it, and are afflicted by it."

"Yeah," he said. "That's part of the shattering impact of McGinniss's book. People who have read it feel that they know me, that they have got inside my head. That's the evilness—I don't know any other word—of his concocted scenario. He's crafted it well enough, and it appears to be very deep. But he was crafting facts to fit an opinion. He wasn't crafting his opinion to fit the facts."

I asked MacDonald about his life in prison, and he spoke for twenty minutes on the subject. You ask this man a question and he *answers* it. After my return to New York, and for the next eight months, I experienced—as McGinniss had experienced—MacDonald's exhaustive and relentless responsiveness. The briefest and slightest of inquiries on my part would bring twenty-page replies from MacDonald, and huge packages of corroborating documents. MacDonald does nothing by halves, and, just as McGinniss had felt oppressed by the quantity of extraneous details in MacDonald's tapes, so was I oppressed by the mountain of documents that formed in my office. I have read little of the material he has sent—trial transcripts, motions, declarations, affidavits, reports. A document arrives, I glance at it, see words like "bloody syringe," "blue threads," "left chest puncture," "unidentified fingerprints," "Kimberly's urine," and add it to the pile. I know I cannot learn anything about MacDonald's guilt or innocence from this material. It is like looking for proof or disproof of the existence of God in a flower—it all depends on how you read the evidence. If you start out with a presumption of his guilt, you read the documents one way, and another way if you presume his innocence. The material does not "speak for itself."

Similarly, how one "reads" MacDonald himself depends on one's prior assumption of what he did or didn't do on the night of February 17, 1970. Dr. Stone, assuming MacDonald to be the murderer, sees him as a remorseless psychopath whose eyes can bore holes through tanks. MacDonald's friends and defenders, imagining drug-crazed intruders as the killers, see him as a sort of Hallmark Job. Interestingly, anyone who has adopted neither position—who finds *both* scenarios unimaginable—tends to give MacDonald the benefit of the doubt. To disbelieve what a person says goes against all our instincts. We tend to believe each other.

By his own testimony, McGinniss, when he first met MacDonald, was in this state of benignant skepticism, but in the course of the criminal trial he came to disbelieve MacDonald and to accept—as did the jury and the judge and the other journalists present—the prosecution's theory: that MacDonald killed his wife and his older child during an argument, and then cold-bloodedly killed his younger child to make it seem that there had been a Manson-like massacre. The circumstantial evidence the government produced was ineffectively responded to by the defense; MacDonald was simply unable to explain the discrepancies between his story and the testimony of the physical evidence. In *Fatal Vision*, McGinniss reports that several of the jurors were crying when they returned the verdict. They had not wanted to convict MacDonald but felt they had no choice. One of the jurors told McGinniss of a crucial turning point in his thinking: the playing of a tape recording of an interview of MacDonald by Army investigators, made in April 1970. McGinniss writes in his book: " 'Until I heard that,' a juror would comment later, 'there was no doubt in my mind about his innocence. *All the evidence had just seemed confusing*. But hearing him turned the whole thing around. I began to look at everything in a whole new way. *There was something about the sound of his voice*. A kind of hesitation. He just didn't sound like a man telling the truth. Besides, I don't think someone who just lost his wife the way he said he did would have sat there and complained that her kitchen drawers had been a mess.' " (The italics are mine.)

On such things verdicts hinge. The evidence—as the prosecution put it, the "things that don't lie"—had "just seemed confusing." When I spoke to the McGinniss-trial jurors, they had been similarly susceptible to their impressions of the defendant. Except for Lucille Dillon, all of them "felt" that McGinniss was not telling the truth. "Throughout the whole thing, I kept thinking, You're lying," an alternate juror, Jackie Beria, told me. The jury foreman, Elizabeth Lane, a retired social worker, said, "It was always 'I can't recall,' 'I don't remember,' 'I don't know.' " She added, "I feel bad about the whole thing, because I thought *Fatal Vision* was a very good book. I know how hard it is to get a book together, and how much research he did. I eventually found myself in a position I didn't want to be in, and that was agreeing that MacDonald had a cause for complaint. I had always felt that convicted murderers shouldn't make money out of books and talk shows, and if they do make money it should be sent to the victims. That's where I was coming from. So it wasn't easy for me to see that there was some merit in

MacDonald's suit. Then we saw all those letters. But what bothered me most was that after Buckley and Wambaugh had testified and said that it's perfectly all right to behave this way—that authors do it all the time—McGinniss couldn't stand up and say, 'Yes, I led him on, yes, I lied to him, yes, I deceived him, because we're all agreed in the publishing world that it's O.K. to do this, and it has to be done sometimes, and I did it because I had this book to write, and the book was the most important thing to me, and therefore the means to this end were justified.' He could not stand up in court and say that. He had to pretend he wasn't sure, though the evidence showed he was writing one thing to MacDonald and in fact thinking and believing and saying another thing to other people. Now, that may not be illegal, but it sure is unethical, and it didn't sit well with us, especially when he tried to lie about it." The jurors also told me that they left the trial convinced that MacDonald was guilty. When I asked them why they thought so, they said that after reading *Fatal Vision* (which they had been assigned to do by the judge) they couldn't think anything else: Bostwick's attempts to cast doubt on the book's veracity had evidently not succeeded. (If it says so in a book, it must be true.) Nevertheless (perhaps because of the flatness of McGinniss's portrayal of the murdered wife and children; one never cares about them the way one cares about the victims in Truman Capote's *In Cold Blood*), the jury declined to put MacDonald beyond the pale of sympathy, where Kornstein sought to place him. Rather, they heeded Bostwick's rhetorical question: "Do you think that a person who's been convicted, and believes he's been wrongly convicted, cannot be hurt? Is that conceivable? That's what Mr. Kornstein would have you believe when he calls him a convicted murderer."

IN THE course of preparing his book about a murderer who stubbornly refused to exhibit any of the traits one associates with people who kill, and whose past seemed to yield up nothing more ominous than a banal history of promiscuity, McGinniss finally struck gold. One of MacDonald's friends—she was one of many people MacDonald had urged McGinniss to see—betrayed him. She was a married older woman, with whom MacDonald had had a love affair, and after going to see her McGinniss was able to write this compelling passage:

> I learned also that later that summer, not long after MacDonald had taken up residence in Huntington Beach [it was the summer after the Army hearing exonerated him], he received a visit from a close friend of his mother's—a woman he had known since childhood. She brought with her her ten-year-old son.
>
> During the course of the visit, which extended over a period of weeks, Jeffrey MacDonald became sexually intimate with his mother's friend. He himself had told me about this during one of my visits to Terminal Island. Later, in another part of the country, I located the woman and she confirmed that the story was true, though she was a bit chagrined that he had chosen to make me aware of it.
>
> I asked her what caused her to terminate the relationship, expecting her to say either that finally the impropriety of the situation had started to bother her, or simply that summer was ending and it was time to go home.

Instead, she said she had left abruptly—before she had planned to—because of two incidents involving her ten-year-old son. The first, she said, occurred when MacDonald—angered by the boy's misbehavior inside his apartment—had carried him outside and dangled him by the feet over the edge of the dock, threatening to drop him head first into the water.

The second incident, the woman said, had occurred later in the summer when she, Jeff, and her son were out for a cruise on his boat. Again, the boy had done something to anger MacDonald. This time, the woman said, MacDonald had grabbed the boy and had told him, in an even more furious and more threatening tone, that upon returning to shore he was going to take the boy's head and hold it over the front of the boat and crush his skull against the dock.

Eventually I spoke to the boy—now a young adult attending an Ivy League college—about his recollection of these incidents. . . .

[He] said the first incident had not been unduly alarming. Perhaps just a form of roughhousing that had gone a little too far. But the second episode—the scene on the boat—he said, "I remember with real terror to this day." He could not recall what in particular he had done to so anger MacDonald, "but he came at me, yelling, and I remember kind of a fire in his eyes. It *really, really* was scary. I didn't know what he was going to do. In fact, what he did was to throw me in the water—he threw me off the side of the boat while it was moving and I can remember actually feeling relieved that he hadn't done anything more.

"But I will never forget it. I will never forget that look in his eyes. You know, maybe as a kid you perceive things more directly, in a way, than you do as an adult. But ever since that moment on the boat I believed that he must have been guilty. Just from seeing that kind of fire in his eyes.

And I did not want to stay around him anymore. I was very frightened and I told my mother I wanted to go home right away. And we did."

The passage stands out in the book. It is the single, indelible instance of murderous rage on MacDonald's part. When Mike Wallace, in his interview for "60 Minutes," confronted MacDonald with McGinniss's book, this was one of the passages he read to him. MacDonald sputtered out a denial ("That never happened. It's a lie") and then dispatched Ray Shedlick to get a retraction from the mother, her husband, and the boy. But the retraction was not forthcoming. Something evidently *had* happened on the boat to upset the boy and to cause his mother, ten years later, to talk about it to a journalist. In a letter she wrote to MacDonald a few months after she saw McGinniss, she said of the interview, "He turned out to be very easy to talk to, charming and disarming. He, of course, is your devoted fan and supporter, but I think he is having a struggle with the book. I guess all good writers have labor pains." Interestingly, the mother and MacDonald have continued in friendly correspondence. All his anger is directed at McGinniss. When I questioned MacDonald about the incident in a letter, he replied, "What McGinniss is saying is 'Yes, I'm aware no one has ever seen or heard of Jeff MacDonald being violent—except, of course, for a few seconds on Feb. 17, 1970—but I, Joe McGinniss, super-important author, have discovered the one other time Jeff MacDonald's latent violence was uncovered.' . . . McGinniss had to depict me that way to justify his Judas-style of friendship, and so he simply takes normal events and concocts evil in them." In the same letter, MacDonald described his idyllic relationship with the boy, writing of the amiable horseplay that went on between them ("I would be fishing at the end of my dock, and he would sneak up behind me & push me in & run away with glee. In return, I'd push him in whenever possible"), and speculating on the possible psychological motives for the boy's "misconception or misperception of horseplay, or an attempt at discipline." I was already familiar with MacDonald's version of the incident, having read Bob Keeler's interview with him in the blue loose-leaf book. The interview took place two months after the Mike Wallace taping, and, again, MacDonald vehemently repudiated the passage. "O.K., she and I developed this relationship," he told Keeler. "There's no question the husband was cuckolded, and I feel terrible about what I did. But that does not make what Joe wrote accurate. That's an absolute fabrication. That never occurred."

Keeler had then called up the mother and said, "I wonder if you could tell me, first of all, did those things occur the way McGinniss wrote them in the book."

"Yes, they did," the mother replied. "The first incident was more in jest. The second one I didn't like at all, though I didn't realize my son was so frightened."

"But as far as the passage in the book goes, does that sound like an accurate representation of what you told Joe when you talked to him?"

"Yes. The two incidents happened, though I don't think that made a killer of Jeff, and I wasn't so frightened that I thought My God! I just thought—like you would if you were staying in somebody's house and they gave you a very unpleasant answer—We've been here too long, it's time to go home. It was no more than that, but apparently my son was alarmed by it."

At the depositions of McGinniss and MacDonald taken

by opposing counsel, each lawyer worried the boy-in-the-boat incident and searched it for an advantage to his side; and each finally decided to pretty much leave it alone at trial. The incident is another illustration of the difficulty of knowing the truth about anything. One could spend years studying it, as investigators spent years working over the MacDonald murders, and end up with no certain answer to the question of what "really" happened. In this case, however, the question is not who committed the crime but whether a crime was committed at all. As Dr. Stone's lively imagination invested the features of a man he had glimpsed in a courtroom with the look of monstrous evil, so might the boy's nervous fancy (he knew that MacDonald had been accused of killing children) have invested an innocent rebuke with murderous intent. On the other hand, the boy might have sensed something actually dangerous in MacDonald. Only if MacDonald should confess to the murders, or if someone else should be revealed as the murderer, will we come any closer to being able to judge what happened in the boat.

THE dinner I had with Michael Malley in the spring of 1988 had come about at MacDonald's urging. Malley had been an excellent plaintiff's witness at the McGinniss trial, testifying about relations between McGinniss and MacDonald at the Kappa Alpha house in Raleigh in a most lucid and evenhanded-sounding matter. "How many hours a day would you estimate you saw them together?" Bostwick asked him.

A: I would say on a typical day it was an hour in the morning, before court, and three or four hours in the evening. Not always exclusively, but Joe was around. He was always around Jeff; not always but most of the time he was around Jeff.

Q: Did it concern you that he was spending too much time with Dr. MacDonald?

A: No.

Q: Did it relieve you?

A: Yes.

Q: Why?

A: Well, at some point I didn't want to be the only reservoir of sympathy that Jeff had. At Fort Bragg [at the Army hearing], sometimes—because Bernie wasn't there, and Jim Douthat, the other military lawyer, went home at night—sometimes I spent two or three hours an evening with Jeff. And while it certainly tightened our friendship, it was also very, very hard on me. And I didn't want to go through that again in North Carolina—that he would have only me to talk to. And Joe filled the bill nicely. I mean, he and Jeff wound up, from my observation, being as close as Jeff and I were at Fort Bragg. So they had each other to talk to, and I could concentrate on what I was trying to do. I mean, I didn't back off from Jeff, but I wasn't there to be a friend.

Later, Bostwick asked Malley, "You still consider yourself a friend of Dr. MacDonald?"

A: Yes.

Q: Do you still consider yourself a friend of Mr. McGinniss?

A: Today?

Q: Yes.

A: It's a very hard question to answer. You know, Joe has never done anything to me personally, so I can't say that he has ever personally offended me; but I certainly was absolutely outraged at the book. I consider that to be a real detriment to our friendship.

Q: Well, what was it about the book that you considered, let us say, outrageous?

A: Primarily two things. One is his portrait of Jeff, which I believe to be wrong. I mean, just Jeff's personality. And the other is the putting forward of a motive or a method by which Jeff would have done this—this drug-induced craziness, which, from everything I know, is so contrary to what the facts really are. To me, it's just made up. And I consider that to be a serious, serious impediment to friendship.

Malley did equally well under Kornstein's cross-examination:

Q: Now, you are a lawyer, Mr. Malley. When you went to the Harvard Law School, they still taught about the First Amendment, didn't they?

A: Do they not anymore? Yes, sir, they did. . . .

Q: Mr. Malley, isn't this attempt by the plaintiff, to punish an author for writing a book, the equivalent of book burning?

A: No, sir, it is not.

MALLEY is an attractive, fit, bearded man of forty-seven with a very charming smile and an atmosphere of obscure difficulty, unease, and unhappiness about him. When, near the end of the evening, he told me that Conrad was his favorite writer, I realized that Malley himself, in his mysterious desperation, was a character out of Conrad. He had written an extraordinary review of *Fatal Vision* in 1984 for the *Princeton Alumni Weekly*, in which he asked, and tried to answer, the question of "how McGinniss came to detest Jeff enough to write this book." Malley concluded:

What McGinniss finally does not like is Jeff's unthinking acceptance of middle-class values and middle-class contradictions in morality, sexuality, friendship, finances—the flawed vision of the good life as McGinniss (and Jeff, too) sees it. It is a life which does not lend itself to the heroes McGinniss says he wants. It is a life he feels free to condemn and betray, just as in all his books he condemns and betrays the friends who gave him their confidences and their lives. Yet he is uneasy in doing this dirty work, because he wants there to be a higher reason for, a meaning in, what he is doing. He wants, ultimately, a forgiveness not for the subjects of his book but for himself.

The irony is that McGinniss's resolution of Jeff's case is relentlessly prosaic, middle-class, and banal—all the things McGinniss seems to detest . . . [It] boils down to the pedestrian "discovery" that Jeff swallowed one too many diet pills and therefore offed his family. In the end, McGinniss's vision is of a middle-class, unerotic pornography. It is as if Marlow discovered in Lord Jim the final truth that Jim's sin was both unexceptional and unredeemable, and Jim was destined and doomed to be a file-clerk prisoner in an obscure shipping office.

Now, in the dimly lit restaurant, like Marlow speaking of Jim to an interlocutor on a starlit tropical veranda, Malley spoke to me of MacDonald. He said, "If you marshal the government's evidence and if you marshal our evidence, it is not clear what happened. Jeff has his story, but he doesn't have all the details, by his own admission. What it comes down to is that he is the only eyewitness, and he looks you in the eye and says, 'I didn't do it.' I believe him. I wound up believing him the way Joe wound up not believing him. Jeff convinced me he was telling the truth in 1970, when the case was fresh and new and didn't have twenty years of lawyers' argument and regurgitation and refinement. In 1970, I was in a position to know whatever there was to know, and there isn't much new evidence. In 1970, it was fresh and new to me, and I had to make up my mind. I decided the evidence didn't point to Jeff. It didn't point away from him, either. But he was believable, and I trusted him, and I still do. My own guess is that the Army's decision to drop charges was also based on trusting what somebody said. That's how I made up my mind, and I have never had any particular reason to change it."

Malley talked about the people who have taken up MacDonald as a cause. "It's easy to have a cause when the cause is so likable—it's sort of like being for homeless puppies. Jeff has changed a lot, to my way of thinking. Partly, I've changed a lot, too. But Jeff used to be much more likable. He didn't have the sort of persona he now almost consciously puts on. He used to be a pretty naïve guy. This experience has taught him a lot, and it's not for the better, though you can't blame him."

"What is worse about him?"

"What's worse about him is that he's become not only a real, a physical, prisoner but a prisoner of his case and of his image and of what people expect of him. And he's become a prisoner of the publicity—which is, most of all, McGinniss's book. Jeff now judges his words and his actions by what people who have read the book will think of him, and what he can do to undo that impression. It's not spontaneous. Jeff is not an open, friendly person anymore. And he used to be. We were not particular friends in college—we became close only after I got into the case—because I've never been that way myself. I like people like that, but I myself have never been open and friendly and talked to people on the street and made friends easily. He always did, and after a while you get to like that. Now he's much more—'guarded' isn't the right word, but it's close. Many people don't realize that. They think he's still open and friendly and outgoing. But now there is a method to it. I think it's very conscious. It has to be. He can't do anything for himself, so he has to manipulate the people around him. He's not able to be a spontaneous guy anymore. He's very thoughtful about what he says and does. In one sense, that's a good thing. It's maturity. But in terms of old-time friendship it's also a little disconcerting to see that happen.

"I still count Jeff as one of my best friends, but Jeff knows that I don't need him and that he needs me. It didn't use to be that way. It used to be that neither of us needed the other. Now it's pretty clear that he needs me for certain things, and that he has no control over whether I do them or not. When I visit him, I am always struck—and maybe it's because I'm in this little, small room, and they bring him in in handcuffs—by how our role-playing situation has changed. When Jeff used to take me out on his boat, he was in charge—he drove the boat, and I had the beer in my hand. It's much different now, and he plays it much differently. I don't blame him. But it's also not very pleasant. I've never liked relationships where someone wanted something from me. I like relationships that are two-sided. And this isn't two-sided anymore. Jeff doesn't have anything to offer me—besides his friendship. I think there's a sincere liking for me on Jeff's part, and it's certainly reciprocated, but liking isn't enough anymore. Jeff doesn't need people to like him—he needs people to like him *and* do something for him. That's one of the problems of being a lawyer—and, I suppose, a writer. You're one of the people that Jeff makes a pitch to. Jeff made a pitch to Joe. He probably made a pitch to you—not just to like him but to do something for him."

As Malley talked, he sounded, chillingly, like a man talking about a woman he once loved but now finds pathetic. Why was he telling me this?

I said, "Why do people let journalists write about them?"

Malley said, "In Jeff's case, there was the obvious self-serving motive: he wanted a book that would tell the world he was innocent and a nice guy. But at some point the world's opinion became secondary, and the real audience for Jeff's ego became Joe. Jeff really liked Joe, and he really trusted Joe. And that's why it was such an incredible betrayal. If the book had said, 'I reluctantly came to the conclusion that this nice guy, whom I really liked, killed his wife and children,' that would have been one thing. But the book says, 'This guy is a cold-blooded killer, a cold-blooded manipulator, a cold-blooded liar, and only I, Joe McGinniss, saw through it from the very beginning, but I had to be sure.' I always knew that Joe had the option of not believing Jeff, and Jeff knew that, too, but what I didn't know was that Joe had the option of disliking Jeff. And Joe not only never gave a hint that this was the way he felt but did just the opposite: he gave every indication that he liked Jeff. He was this little macho buddy of Jeff's. They ran together, they swapped girl stories together, they did all this macho stuff together."

A little later, Malley said, "On some level, I sympathize with Joe. I don't think Joe cynically said to himself, 'I believe he is innocent, but that won't sell my book, so I'll say he's guilty.' I don't believe that; I've never believed that."

"The flaw in McGinniss's character may be that he doesn't know how to be anything but ingratiating."

"That's right. I think Joe, more than anything else in life, wants to be liked. In that sense, he's very much like Jeff. But, unlike Jeff, Joe also wants to pass judgment on everything. Joe is a very judgmental guy, though it's not obvious when you talk to him, because he has this attitude of eternal tolerance."

"If Joe had said, 'Look, Jeff, I have come to believe that you did it,' would Jeff have gone on talking to him?"

"Yes, I think he would have. He would have refused to believe that Joe was not persuadable."

Malley spoke of MacDonald's adaptability: "He didn't want to spend the rest of his life in mourning or in hunting the killers. Now he accepts prison as he accepted the murders."

"It's a ruined life."

"Yes, it is. Jeff's life has been dominated by this since he was twenty-six, and unless something dramatic happens he won't get out of prison until the end of the century. It's unlikely that he will get a new trial. The system has run its course."

I CORRESPONDED with MacDonald between January and November of 1988. He wrote me long letters on lined legal-pad sheets, and I wrote him short typewritten letters. A correspondence is a kind of love affair. It takes place in a small, closed, private space—a sheet of paper within an envelope is its vehicle and emblem—and it is tinged by a subtle but palpable eroticism. When we write to someone regularly, we begin to look forward to his letters and to feel increasing emotion at the sight of the familiar envelope. But if we are honest with ourselves we will acknowledge that the chief pleasure of the correspondence lies in its responsive aspect rather than in its receptive one. It is with our own epistolary persona that we fall in love, rather than with that of our pen pal; what makes the arrival of a letter a momentous event is the occasion it affords for writing rather than for reading. Some of the mystery of McGinniss's letters to MacDonald lifted for me when I stepped into McGinniss's shoes and, as it were, retrod the terrain of his fatal correspondence. Of course, I avoided the obvious pitfalls that had caused him so much misery in court—I promised MacDonald nothing, and I wrote nothing about myself that I would mind anyone else's knowing—but as I now peruse the Xeroxes I made of my letters to MacDonald I see that I was no less enamored of the sound of my voice than McGinniss had been of his. As McGinniss had played the dual role of celebrity author and macho buddy to MacDonald, so I enacted the part of a sort of Lady Bountiful of journalism, writing to this poor convict and letting him understand how fortunate he was to know me and to be reading my aperçus about the writer-subject relationship. In their way, I find my letters as unpleasant as McGinniss's. It is not so much what they say that bothers me as their self-satisfied tone and their fundamental falseness—the falseness that is built into the writer-subject relationship, and about which nothing can be done. Only when a subject breaks off relations with the writer—as McGinniss broke off relations with me—is the journalist in a completely uncompromised position. Unlike other relationships that have a purpose beyond themselves and are clearly delineated as such (dentist-patient, lawyer-client, teacher-student), the writer-subject relationship seems to depend for its life on a kind of fuzziness and murkiness, if not utter covertness, of purpose. If everybody put his cards on the table, the game would be over. The journalist must do his work in a kind of deliberately induced state of moral anarchy. This is what Buckley and Wambaugh were trying to say in court, and if they had put it less arrogantly and more apologetically—if they had put it as a baffling and unfortunate occupational hazard rather than as a virtuous necessity—they might not have antagonized the jury as they did.

The subject's side of the equation is not without its moral problems, either. In their way, MacDonald's letters to me were as false as mine to him. He was making his pitch to me just as Malley had described it, and was no less intent on "using" me than I was intent on "using" him. Although I tried not to trifle with his hopes, I could see that he never let go of his fantasy that I would write the "decent man in prison" narrative that McGinniss had not written; his twenty- or thirty-page letters were all directed toward that purpose, and were like sledgehammer strokes in their relentless, repetitive, bombastic self-justification. When a letter came, I would put off reading it—the writing was unrelievedly windy—but when I finally read it something unexpected would happen. I would find myself shaken and moved, sometimes to the point of tears. A terrible starkness and bottom-of-life direness permeated these unutterably boring letters that was like the obliterating reality of the paintings of Francis Bacon. Nevertheless, once I began writing this chronicle, I lost my desire to correspond with MacDonald. He had (once again) become a character in a text, and his existence as a real person grew dim for me (as it had grown dim for McGinniss, until MacDonald's lawsuit brought it back into glaring incandescence). A long letter from him lies unanswered on my desk. It tells me about developments in his criminal case—"extraordinarily powerful new evidence," which he is "not yet free to make public," but which he will send me if I want it. I do not want it. If MacDonald has nothing to lose anymore from his encounters with writers, a writer has little to gain from him. The story of the murders has been told—by Joe McGinniss—and it has acquired the aura of a definitive narrative. Should MacDonald actually get a new trial, and even turn out to be innocent, he will be able to rebuild his life, but he will not be able to efface McGinniss's story—any more than "powerful new evidence" of Raskolnikov's innocence would efface Dostoevsky's fable. (Jeffrey Elliot recently abandoned his book about the MacDonald case—no publisher would touch it.) It is all too natural for people who have been wronged or humiliated—or feel they have been—to harbor the fantasy that a writer will come along on a white steed and put everything to rights. As *MacDonald v. McGinniss* illustrates, the writer who comes along is apt to only make things worse. What gives journalism its authenticity and vitality is the tension between the subject's blind self-absorption and the journalist's skepticism. Journalists who swallow the subject's account whole and publish it are not journalists but publicists. If the lesson of *MacDonald v. McGinniss* were taken to heart by prospective subjects, it could indeed, as Kornstein maintained, be the end of journalism. Fortunately for readers and writers alike (as Kornstein's own fantasy-laden letter demonstrates), human nature guarantees that willing subjects will never be in short supply. Like the young Aztec men and women selected for sacrifice, who lived in delightful ease and luxury until the appointed day when their hearts were to be carved from their chests, journalistic subjects know all too well what awaits them when the days of wine and roses—the days of the interviews—are over. And still they say yes whan a journalist calls, and still they are astonished when they see the flash of the knife.

Afterword

ALTHOUGH writers and publishers like to grumble about the proliferation of libel lawsuits in this country, few would seriously propose that anything be done to reverse the trend. The Ayatollah's death sentence on Salman Rushdie brings into relief the primitive feeling that lies behind every libel suit, and makes the writer only too grateful for the mechanism the law provides for transforming the displeased subject's impulse to kill him into the move civilized aim of extracting large sums of money from him. Although the money is rarely collected—most libel suits end in defeat for the plaintiff or in a modest settlement—the lawsuit itself functions as a powerful therapeutic agent, ridding the subject of his feelings of humiliating powerlessness and restoring to him his cheer and *amour propre*. From the lawyer who takes him into his care he immediately receives the relief that a sympathetic hearing of one's grievances affords. Conventional psychotherapy would soon veer off into an unpleasurable examination of the holes in one's story, but the law cure never ceases to be gratifying; in fact, what the lawyer says and writes on his client's behalf is gratifying beyond the latter's wildest expectations. The rhetoric of advocacy law is the rhetoric of the late-night vengeful brooding which in life rarely survives the skeptical light of morning but in a lawsuit becomes inscribed, as if in stone, in the bellicose documents that accrue while the lawsuit takes its course, and proclaims with every sentence "I am right! I am right! I am right!" On the other side, meanwhile, the same orgy of self-justification is taking place. The libel defendant, after an initial anxious moment (we all feel guilty of something, and being sued stirs the feeling up), comes to see, through the ministrations of *his* lawyer-therapist, that he is completely in the right and has nothing to fear. Of pleasurable reading experiences there may be none greater than that afforded by a legal document written on one's behalf. A lawyer will argue for you as you could never argue for yourself, and, with his lawyer's rhetoric, give you a feeling of certitude that you could never obtain for yourself from the language of everyday discourse. People who have never sued anyone or been sued have missed a narcissistic pleasure that is not quite like any other.

A few years ago, I had the opportunity to experience this pleasure when I was sued for libel by the main character of my book *In the Freud Archives*, Jeffrey Masson. I remember well the pile of documents from the lawsuit that collected in my office, to which I would be drawn as if to a forbidden treat, and which I would peruse like a child reading a favorite fairy story over and over again. Of course, my enraptured reading involved only half the documents in the pile—those that had been written by my lawyers. The other half—written by Masson's lawyers— were of no interest; I scanned each item as it arrived, always quickly perceived its weakness and pointlessness, and never looked at it again. On his side, I am sure that Masson did the same thing. In life, it is hard enough to see another person's view of things; in a lawsuit, it is impossible. The fatal attraction of a lawsuit—as Dickens showed us in *Bleak House*, with the case of *Jarndyce v. Jarndyce*—is

the infinite scope it offers for escape from the real world of
ambiguity, obscurity, doubt, disappointment, compro-
mise, and accommodation. The world of the lawsuit is the
world of the Platonic ideal, where all is clear, etched, one
thing or the other. It is a world—as Dickens showed with
his allegory of obsession—that we enter at our peril, since
it is also the world of madness. A few months into the
Masson lawsuit, I took Dickens's warning and drew back
from the brink, returning to it only once again: In the
summer of 1987, when a federal judge summarily dismissed Masson's suit, I'm afraid I found myself reading
and rereading the judge's twenty-seven-page order with
the old solipsistic rapture. But my feeling of low gloating
was soon replaced by a certain weary sympathy for the
man whose efforts had come to nothing.*

Being sued by a person who inhabits the pages of a book
you have written is not, after all, the same as being sued
by someone who exists only in life. You know your adversary more intimately than you know most merely real
people—not only because you have had occasion to study
him more closely than one studies the people one does not
write about, but because you have put a great deal of
yourself into him. *"Madame Bovary, c'est moi,"* Flaubert
said of his famous character. The characters of nonfiction,
no less than those of fiction, derive from the writer's most
idiosyncratic desires and deepest anxieties; they are what
the writer wishes he was and worries that he is. *Masson,
c'est moi.*

* Evidently not yet ready to terminate his law therapy, Masson appealed the
summary judgment. In August 1989, it was upheld by the U.S. Court of
Appeals for the Ninth Circuit in a 2–1 decision. Masson promptly filed yet
another appeal—this one for reconsideration of his case by a larger panel of the
Appeals Court—which is pending as I write.

IN HIS biography of Gogol, Vladimir Nabokov, dismissively citing a theory about the origins of *The Inspector General*, observes:

> It is strange, the morbid inclination we have to derive satisfaction from the fact (usually false and always irrelevant) that a work of art is traceable to a "true story." Is it because we begin to respect ourselves more when we learn that the writer, just like ourselves, was not clever enough to make up a story himself?

When the chronicle of journalistic betrayal which forms the contents of this book was first published in *The New Yorker*, certain members of the journalistic community contended that I had not "made up" my story—that is, had not acted in good faith in presenting it as a new story—but had simply served up a disguised version of the Masson-Malcolm lawsuit. My suggestion that all journalists feel, or should feel, some compunction about the exploitive character of the journalist-subject relationship was held up as a covert confession of the wrong I had done Jeffrey Masson—who was promptly harnessed into the project of showing my text to be nothing but the product of a guilty conscience. The feeling of sympathy for Masson that had been aroused in me by the summary judgment was reawakened by the spectacle of him giving interviews to reporters whose sole interest in him was his usefulness as an agent for the development for their "story behind the story"; once they had used him, they dumped him. The vivid, impudent, complex man who had appeared in my book was sadly diminished in his new literary surroundings. What had they done to complicated, unruly Masson to make him seem so vapid?

However, he served his purpose, and his lawsuit's charge that I had libelled him through misquotation began to circulate in newspapers and magazines throughout the country—not as an accusation, but as an established fact. It is an unnerving experience to pick up the venerable newspaper you have read all your adult life, whose veracity you have never had reason to doubt, and read something about yourself that you know to be untrue.[*] The *Times* published a retraction in due course, but the harm was done. As Tom Wicker recently wrote in his "In the Nation" column, "It's a truism that denials never quite

---

[*] In an article headed "Ethics, Reporters, and the New Yorker," in the March 21, 1989, issue of *The New York Times*, a reporter named Albert Scardino wrote that "testimony at the trial portrayed her as fabricating quotations and manufacturing dialogue," and that "Miss Malcolm conceded the fabrications." Of course, there had never been any such testimony, since there had never been any trial (the suit was dismissed before trial), and, of course, I conceded no fabrications (at the imaginary trial). Some of Scardino's confusion—and that of journalists reporting the subsequent affirming decision of the Appeals Court— doubtless derived from the rather arcane nature of summary judgment, an expedient the law provides for defendants who wish to avoid the expense of a trial. In summary judgment, the defendant must demonstrate that the plaintiff could not possibly win his case at trial. To make this demonstration fit within the confines of Rule 56(c) of the Federal Rules of Civil Procedure—which stipulates that summary judgment may be granted only when "there is no genuine issue as to any material fact"—the defendant is often obliged to leave unchallenged dire accusations which, at trial, the plaintiff would have to back up with evidence. Thus, in the Masson-Malcolm suit, to comply with Rule 56(c), the defense did not challenge the plaintiff's accusation that four pages of notes which I had submitted to the court as the source of certain quotations in my book were "fabrications." Accordingly, the decisions of the lower court and the Appeals Court said, in effect, that even if Masson's accusation regarding the notes were true, his case could not prevail in the face of the evidence of 1,065 undisputed pages of tape transcript. But the "even if" formula of the summary judgment was evidently not grasped by the daily press and was taken to mean "it is so." I would like to say in the congenial shade of this footnote that I consider the accusation that I fabricated notes and invented quotations ludicrous beyond belief, that I utterly deny it, and that there is no evidence for it.

catch up with charges. Honest journalists who may have mistakenly printed false information know that the most prominent retraction never quite undoes the damage done by the original publication." The occasion for Wicker's remark was the death of Owen Lattimore, who had been accused of being a Communist spy by McCarthy, and, after much travail, had succeeded in clearing himself of this and all similar charges. The crux of Wicker's column was this paragraph:

> After his obituary appeared . . . two well-informed people not given to right-wing suspicions told me they were surprised to read that Mr. Lattimore, in fact, had been innocent of the charges. They knew McCarthy exaggerated, but for nearly forty years, as one put it, they had been under the impression that Mr. Lattimore was at least "tainted."

Because of the *Times*'s story, in some well-informed people's minds I, too, will no doubt always be tainted—a kind of fallen woman of journalism.

WHAT is at stake for the reader in the issue of whether or not a writer has violated the rules of his genre? Contemporary fiction, after all, is full of such trespasses. If E. L. Doctorow can experiment with the form of the novel by mixing fictitious characters with historical personages, and if Philip Roth can go so far as to report the death of a character in the first chapter of *The Counterlife* and then, in the second, send the man to Israel to recuperate from the open-heart operation that killed him on page seventeen ("So I lied"), why can't writers of nonfiction fool around in the same way, take similar liberties, conduct their own modernist experiments? Why should the writer in one genre enjoy more privileges than the writer in the other?

The answer is: because the writer of fiction is entitled to more privileges. He is master of his own house and may do what he likes in it; he may even tear it down if he is so inclined (as Roth was inclined in *The Counterlife*). But the writer of nonfiction is only a renter, who must abide by the conditions of his lease, which stipulates that he leave the house—and its name is Actuality—as he found it. He may bring in his own furniture and arrange it as he likes (the so-called New Journalism is about the arrangement of furniture), and he may play his radio quietly. But he must not disturb the house's fundamental structure or tamper with any of its architectural features. The writer of non-fiction is under contract to the reader to limit himself to events that actually occurred and to characters who have counterparts in real life, and he may not embellish the truth about these events or these characters.

I speak about the limitation on a nonfiction writer's scope for invention as if it were a burden, when, in fact, it is what makes his work so much less arduous. Where the novelist has to start from scratch and endure the terrible labor of constructing a world, the nonfiction writer gets his world ready-made. Although it is a world by no means as coherent as the world of fiction, and is peopled by characters by no means as lifelike as the characters in fiction, the reader accepts it without complaint; he feels compensated for the inferiority of his reading experience by what he regards as the edifying character of the genre: a work about something that is true, about events that really occurred and people who actually lived or live, is valued simply for being that, and is read in a more lenient spirit than a work of imaginative literature, from which we expect a more intense experience. The reader extends a kind of credit to the writer of nonfiction which he doesn't extend to the writer of fiction, and for this reason the writer of nonfiction has to be punctilious about delivering the goods for which the reader has prepaid with his forbearance. Of course, there is no such thing as a work of pure factuality, any more than there is one of pure fictitiousness. As every work of fiction draws on life, so every work of nonfiction draws on art. As the novelist must curb his imagination in order to keep his text grounded in the common experience of man (dreams exemplify the uncurbed imagination—thus their uninterestingness to everyone but their author), so the journalist must temper his literal-mindedness with the narrative devices of imaginative literature.

One of the striking instances of the necessity for this mediation—showing how the literally true may actually be a kind of falsification of reality—is offered by a transcript of tape-recorded speech. When we talk with somebody, we are not aware of the strangeness of the language we are speaking. Our ear takes it in as English, and only if we see it transcribed verbatim do we realize that it is a kind of foreign tongue. What the tape recorder has revealed about human speech—that Molière's M. Jourdain was mistaken: we do not, after all, speak in prose—is something like what the nineteenth-century photographer Eadweard Muybridge's motion studies revealed about animal locomotion. Muybridge's fast camera caught and froze positions never before seen, and demonstrated that artists throughout art history had been "wrong" in their renderings of horses (among other animals) in motion. Contemporary artists, at first upset by Muybridge's discoveries, soon regained their equanimity, and continued to render what the eye, rather than the camera, sees. Similarly, novelists of our tape-recorder era have continued to write dialogue in English rather than in tape-recorderese, and most journalists who work with a tape recorder use the transcript of an extended interview merely as an aid to memory—as a sort of second chance at note-taking—rather than as a text for quotation. The transcript is not a finished version, but a kind of rough draft of expression. As everyone who has studied transcripts of tape-recorded speech knows, we all seem to be extremely reluctant to come right out and say what we mean—thus the bizarre syntax, the hesitations, the circumlocutions, the repetitions, the contradictions, the lacunae in almost every non-sentence we speak.

The tape recorder has opened up a sort of underwater world of linguistic phenomena whose Cousteaus are as yet unknown to the general public. (A fascinating early contribution to this field of research is a paper forbiddingly entitled "Countertransference Examples of the Syntactic Expression of Warded-Off Contents" by Hartwig Dahl, Virginia Teller, Donald Moss, and Manuel Truhillo [*Psychoanalytic Quarterly*, 1978], which analyzes the verbatim speech of a psychoanalyst during a session and shows its strange syntax to be a form of covert bullying of the patient.) But this world is not the world of journalistic discourse. When a journalist undertakes to quote a subject he has interviewed on tape, he owes it to the subject, no less than to the reader, to translate his speech into prose. Only the most uncharitable (or inept) journalist will hold a subject to his literal utterances and fail to perform the sort of editing and rewriting that, in life, our ear automatically and instantaneously performs.

For example, when I asked Dr. Michael Stone, a psychiatrist who testified for the defense in the MacDonald-McGinniss lawsuit, if he thought there was any possibility that MacDonald was innocent, he said (on tape):

No. In fact I had hoped to be able to say—since the judge kind of cheated me out of my opportunity to be redirected—Dan [Daniel Kornstein, the defense lawyer] said I had time to be redirected—then Bostwick cleverly ate up all the time with a bunch of silly questions so that—the judge just let him go on and on—and then finally there wasn't really time because I had to catch a plane at a certain hour. However, the material I gave to Kornfeld, was that having looked at all this and having slept on this material the night after my first appearance at trial, I had a kind of insight, if you will, that the four intruders represented, psychologically speaking, the only truthful thing that MacDonald had told—that there *were* really four intruders—but, of course, they weren't exactly as he depicted them—but there were four people who intruded upon the hedonistic—and—life style and whoring around of Jeff MacDonald—and four people who, you know, intruded into his disinclination to be a responsible husband and father, namely Colette, Kristy, Kimberly, and the unborn son.

In my text I rendered this as:

No. In fact—and this, too, was something I wasn't able to say in court, since Bostwick cleverly ate up all the time with a bunch of silly questions and I had to catch a plane—the four intruders who MacDonald claimed were responsible for the murders represented the only truth, psychologically speaking, that he told. There really *were* four people who intruded on the hedonistic life style and whoring around of Jeff Mac-

Donald: the four people who intruded on his disinclination to be a responsible husband and father; namely, Colette, Kristen, Kimberly, and the unborn son.

Before the invention of the tape recorder, no quotation could be verbatim—what Boswell quotes Dr. Johnson as saying was obviously not precisely what Johnson said; we will never know what that was—and many journalists continue to work without benefit of this double-edged technological aid, doing their work of editing or paraphrasing on the spot, as they scribble in their notebooks. In this litigious time, it has proved useful for journalists to have an electronic record of what a subject said. But this extra-literary reason for using a tape recorder, as well as the more conventional one of capturing the flavor of a subject's speech, may prove to be insufficiently beneficial—to both text and journalist—to warrant the continued use of the tape recorder in journalistic interviews. Texts containing dialogue and monologue derived from a tape—however well edited the transcript may be—tend to retain some trace of their origin (almost a kind of metallic flavor) and lack the atmosphere of truthfulness present in work where it is the writer's own ear that has caught the drift of the subject's thought. And lawsuits in which transcripts of tape-recorded interviews are used to settle the question of what a subject did or didn't say can degenerate (as, in my opinion, *Masson v. Malcolm* degenerated) into farcical squabbles about the degree to which a journalist may function as a writer rather than as a stenographer.

The quotations in this book—and in my other journalistic writings—are not, for the reasons given, identical to their speech counterparts. Neither, however, are any of them of the "probable" variety described by Joseph Wambaugh. Although the Wambaugh technique is frequently used in historical novels—"*Mon dieu,*" Richelieu said, "when the King hears this, he will freak out!"—as well as in Wambaugh's own "true crime" novels, it is out of the question for works that represent themselves as journalism. When we read a quotation in a newspaper story or in a text such as this one, we assume it to be a rendering of what the speaker actually—not probably—said. The idea of a reporter inventing rather than reporting speech is a repugnant, even sinister, one. Because so much of our knowledge of the world derives from what we read in the press, we naturally become nervous whenever the question of misquotation is raised. Fidelity to the subject's thought and to his characteristic way of expressing himself is the sine qua non of journalistic quotation—one under which all stylistic considerations are subsumed. Fortunately for reader and subject alike, the relatively minor task of translating tape-recorderese into English and the major responsibility of trustworthy quotation are in no way inimical; in fact, as I have proposed (and over and over again have discovered for myself), they are fundamentally and decisively complementary.

I HAVE been writing long pieces of reportage for a little over a decade. Almost from the start, I was struck by the unhealthiness of the journalist-subject relationship, and every piece I wrote only deepened my consciousness of the canker that lies at the heart of the rose of journalism. When Daniel Kornstein and Joe McGinniss approached me with their larger-than-life example of the journalist-subject problem—a lawsuit in which a man serving a prison sentence for murder sues the writer who uneasily

deceived him for four years—it dovetailed with the thinking on the subject I had been doing for many years and
fired my imagination with its narrative possibilities. The
notion that my account of this case is a thinly veiled account of my own experience of being sued by a subject not
only is wrong but betrays a curious naïveté about the
psychology of journalists. The dominant and most deep-
dyed trait of the journalist is his timorousness. Where the
novelist fearlessly plunges into the water of self-exposure,
the journalist stands trembling on the shore in his beach
robe. Not for him the strenuous athleticism—which is the
novelist's daily task—of laying out his deepest griefs and
shames before the world. The journalist confines himself
to the clean, gentlemanly work of exposing the griefs and
shames of others. Precisely because MacDonald's lawsuit
had no elements in common with Masson's did I feel em-
boldened to write about it (and, incidentally, was I, as a
defendant, able to position myself so as to view a plaintiff's case with sympathy). *MacDonald v. McGinniss* was
unprecedented in being concerned with a writer's personal
conduct toward his subject—no previous lawsuit had
opened this messy drawer; *Masson v. Malcolm* was confined
to a published text. That some readers were nevertheless
able to think of the present book as being veiled autobiography (and thus found my text incomplete, even
devious, because it did not mention the Masson lawsuit)
derives, I have come to think, from a misconception about
the identity of the character called "I" in a work of journalism. This character is unlike all the journalist's other
characters in that he forms the exception to the rule that
nothing may be invented: the "I" character in journalism
is almost pure invention. Unlike the "I" of autobiography,
who is meant to be seen as a representation of the writer,

the "I" of journalism is connected to the writer only in a tenuous way—the way, say, that Superman is connected to Clark Kent. The journalistic "I" is an overreliable narrator, a functionary to whom crucial tasks of narration and argument and tone have been entrusted, an ad hoc creation, like the chorus of Greek tragedy. He is an emblematic figure, an embodiment of the idea of the dispassionate observer of life. Nevertheless, readers who readily accept the idea that the narrator in a work of fiction is not the same person as the author of the book will stubbornly resist the idea of the invented "I" of journalism; and even among journalists, there are those who have trouble sorting themselves out from the Supermen of their texts. There was a moment in my conversation with the professor-journalist Jeffrey Elliot when this confusion was brought into sharp relief. Elliot told me of his outrage over an incident in *Fatal Vision*—one which also appeared in the film version of the book—in which MacDonald and the members of his defense team in Raleigh entertained themselves during a birthday party for Bernie Segal by throwing darts at an enlarged photograph of Brian Murtagh, an abrasive government prosecutor. McGinniss wrote:

> One by one, each member of the defense team took a turn throwing darts at the picture. Jeffrey MacDonald scored a direct hit. He cheered for himself as his attorneys and their assistants clapped and laughed. In high spirits, he seemed oblivious to the possibility that, under the circumstances, it might not have been appropriate for him to be propelling a sharp pointed object toward even the photographic representation of a human being.

In the film version, MacDonald is shown throwing darts as Joe McGinniss looks on grimly. At McGinniss's first deposition, Gary Bostwick asked him if he himself had thrown a dart at the party, and McGinniss replied, "I don't recall." At the MacDonald-McGinniss trial, Segal testified that he remembered McGinniss *had* thrown a dart. Elliot said indignantly to me, "How can you write a book and consult on a film where you portray yourself as standing in the corner at a birthday party watching MacDonald throw darts at the face of the prosecutor—standing there looking as if you found this repulsive—when in actuality you weren't watching aghast but were throwing darts like the rest?" He went on, "It's dishonest. You use that scene to make MacDonald look wicked and evil, and you're this pure character just watching, horrified. But if you participated in the dart-throwing, then don't write the scene. Because it's going to come out that you participated."

"No it isn't," (the actual) I said to Elliot. "Until the MacDonald lawsuit, no one ever thought of challenging a journalist's personal conduct the way Bostwick challenged McGinniss's."

"I'm sure McGinniss didn't think his would be either."

"That's right."

"Well, it's outrageous."

Bostwick's delvings into the discrepancy between the character "I" of *Fatal Vision* and the man who wrote the book are what make the lawsuit unique and give it its subversive character. Kornstein was right to characterize it as a threat to journalism. If the journalist is going to have to start proleptically imitating the behavior of the "pure character" he will become in his text, his hands will be tied. The oxymoronic term "participant observer" was coined to describe the fieldwork of anthropologists and sociologists; and it also describes the fieldwork of journalists. Because McGinniss participated more fully and intensely in the culture of his subject than most journalists have occasion to do—how many of us live with a subject for six weeks, accompany him daily to a murder trial, form a business partnership with him, and write to him in prison for three years?—he was more vulnerable than most of us would be to the charge of duplicity on which Bostwick poised his case. But what McGinniss did egregiously, most journalists do more subtly and quietly. Colleagues have said to me, "I would never do what McGinniss did. I'm not that kind of writer. It would pain me to cause a subject distress"—as if what we *write* is the issue. The moral ambiguity of journalism lies not in its texts but in the relationships out of which they arise— relationships that are invariably and inescapably lopsided. The "good" characters in a piece of journalism are no less a product of the writer's unholy power over another person than are the "bad" ones. During my friendly dealings with Gary Bostwick, I always knew I had the option of writing something about him that would cause him distress, and he knew it, too, which gave our "false friendship" a bracing kind of self-consciousness rare between writers and subjects, but which in no way altered the authoritarian structure of the relationship. He was completely at my mercy. I held all the cards. Yes, he had consented to be written about, and yes, he hoped to gain something from his encounter with me. The fact that the subject may be trying to manipulate the journalist—and none but the most otherworldly of subjects is above at least some manipulativeness—does not offset the journalist's own sins against the libertarian spirit. "Two wrongs don't make a right," as the folksy Bostwick was fond of saying during the trial, quoting his mother. As it happened, Bostwick's personal agenda and my narrative one coincided; if they hadn't, I probably would have put what I believed to be the reader's interests ahead of Bostwick's susceptibilities—though not necessarily: in my time, I, too, have committed the journalistic solecism of putting a person's feelings above a text's necessities.

There is an infinite variety of ways in which journalists struggle with the moral impasse that is the subject of this book. The wisest know that the best they can do—and most practitioners easily avoid the crude and gratuitous two-facedness of the MacDonald-McGinniss case—is still not good enough. The not so wise, in their accustomed manner, choose to believe there is no problem and that they have solved it.

READING CHEKHOV
A Critical Journey

'An excellent book . . . it is a pleasure to read, and it sends you straight back to Chekhov, as it should' A. S. Byatt, *Guardian*

'It is literary pilgrimage, homage, travelogue, biography, literary criticism and a restrained love letter all rolled into one' Neel Mukherjee, *The Times*

'One of the most consistent non-fiction writers of our time. Certainly, she is one of the most brilliant' Sebastian Smee, *Spectator*

'It is impossible to put this book down and not feel that one knows Chekhov much better - and impossible not to want to go and re-read him' Anne Applebaum, *Sunday Telegraph*

PSYCHOANALYSIS
The Impossible Profession

'Malcolm writes wonderfully well…she can't write a boring sentence' John Lanchester, *Daily Telegraph*

The process known as psychoanalysis is sometimes revered, sometimes derided, and most often misunderstood. What good does it do? Can it help anyone? What risks does it pose to both patient and analyst? None of these questions can be easily answered, but in Janet Malcolm's brilliant narrative, their complexity is limpidly revealed.

'Janet Malcolm has managed somehow to peer into the reticent, reclusive world of psychoanalysis and to report to us, with remarkable fidelity, what she has seen. Her book is journalism become art' Joseph Adelson, *New York Times Book Review*

IN THE FREUD ARCHIVES

Who will inherit the secrets of Sigmund Freud? Who will protect his reputation? Who may destroy it?

Janet Malcolm's investigation into the personalities who clash over Freud's legacy is a classic story of seduction and betrayal, love and hatred, fantasy and reality.

'From beginning to end it has the coolly accomplished excitement of a thriller' *Sunday Times*

'In this brilliant and enjoyable book, a major crisis within one of the most important systems of ideas of our century is presented in the style of a movie vehicle for Jack Nicholson' *Times Literary Supplement*